ENDORSEMENTS

In *Threads of the Father,* the very best of Penny comes through and is captured. She is loyal, faithful, kind and encouraging, and you will sense that in each of her writings. As you enjoy the book, take your time. Pour a cup of coffee, take a comfy seat, and prepare to be taken on a journey of enlightenment.

Mike Hayes, DD, Pastor, Author

Penny Renfroe has cultivated a beautiful book of fertile ground, clearly needed by the Church today. This book is a duet; not only between the author and the Lord, but between the heart of the reader and the Holy Spirit. The heavy lifting has been done through the years of Penny's relationship with Jesus. The reader has been given a rare glimpse into what it means to have an intimate, conversational relationship with God the Creator. And importantly, the reader is left with a question, "Now what? How will I apply this to my life? How will this change me?" That is up to you.

Parker Hartzog
Lead Pastor of Era Community Church

Threads of the Father tenderly reveals Penny's intimate conversations with God, welcoming readers into a world where His voice is ever present. Her vulnerability becomes a guiding light, showcasing the simplicity of hearing God in our daily lives. Having known Penny for over a decade, I can confirm that every page echoes her authentic journey. Through her narrative, she paves the way for us, igniting a desire to deepen our relationship with our Creator. Trust me, it will.

Misty deMelo, Founder of DeMelo Group
www.mistydemelo.com

Penny's writings are like a doorway leading us on a journey to capture the time we have with our Heavenly Father. To read these essays is to find Him as He walks with us. Some show us His mind and others reveal His heart. They reveal a sabbath rest in Him. It's a solitude we find in the midst of the busy world we live in. It's true Selah Time. Her book is well worth the read.

John Paty, Author, *The Wilderness of God: The Legacy of the Bride*
and *The Balance of Power: God's Mandate for Multidimensional Living*

Teaching believers how to hear God, recognize His voice, and respond accordingly is one of the greatest gifts we can give Christians today. I am blessed and have the honor of encouraging many to get this book, hear God's voice, and follow Him daily. Thank you, Penny, for hearing God and being obedient to His voice in writing this book!

Pastor Landon Merrill
Bridge Church, wearebridge.church

While reading this book, the overwhelming love of the Father will penetrate your heart. Penny has partnered with God and found such a beautiful way to speak His truths that will bring clarity and healing to any soul. If you have found yourself hungering to hear God's voice, whether in a difficult season or for the first time ever, I greatly recommend this read. I believe you will enjoy the journey it leads you through, and undoubtedly, you'll find God sitting right beside you the entire time.

Cecily C. Williams, Author, *Crystal Pain: God's Etching Through Grief, the Pandemic, and Spiritual Warfare*

I have known Penny Renfroe for years and have worked with her on many occasions. *Threads of the Father* gives the reader a firsthand look into her heart and her conversations with God. She is open to share her desires while also sharing how God answers her with peace, comfort, and provision. This reminds us that we are never alone, and that we, too, can have the same kind of relationship with our Father. This is a must-read for anyone seeking to grow closer in this relationship.

Dave Blaylock, Mayor, Whitesboro, Texas

A book with the genuine power to stir your heart and change the way you communicate with the Father. Rarely can a book do that. *Threads of the Father* unveils the intimate journal between the author, Penny, and our Heavenly Father. Such insight and personal moments shared in such a painterly way, sharing personal experience, so that we may be invited into sweet communion with Jesus Christ and recognize His voice. Don't miss this beautiful book full of short snippets of hope, love, and intimacy with Jesus.

Cynthia Harris

In *Threads of the Father,* Penny Renfroe has lovingly and graciously written and guided us through her own journey of vulnerability with God. Like an industrious weaver, she has pieced together thoughts, words, and poetry to help us dream with God again as He answers our questions and heals our deepest longings. Her creative spirit and kind heart are evident in each page she has crafted with the Creator, to draw us closer, give us peace and grant us assurance that He knows. He sees. He hears. And there is a good plan beyond what we can comprehend. Come along for a journey into wonder. A leap into intimacy with God. I needed this book to slow down and hear, see and just BE again. We all need it. May it heal your heart and impact you forever.

Jill Hellwig
Founder/CEO/Head Coach, Brand New U, LLC
Author, *Grow with Goals*

Threads of the Father

Weaving His Words into our Daily Lives

PENNY RENFROE

Threads of the Father
Weaving His Words into our Daily Lives
Penny Renfroe

To contact the author: penny@pennyrenfroe.com

Library of Congress Control Number: 2024904788
ISBN (Print): 979-8-9894822-5-2
ISBN (E-book): 979-8-9894822-6-9

Published by:

Mary Ethel

Mary Ethel Eckard
Frisco, TX

Cover Concept Design by: Lisa Williams
Simplicity Professional Organizing, timeforsimplicity.com
Illustration 182432348 | Needle Thread © Moonnoom | Dreamstime.com

Dedication

For Rhett and Reese.

May you always have a heart to know the Father,
ears to hear His voice,
and eyes to see Him at work.
May you run with passion after Him!

Contents

Foreword

In John 10:14-15a, Jesus says, *"I am the good shepherd, and I know My own and My own know Me, even as the Father knows Me and I know the Father."* I wonder if the crowd to whom Jesus uttered these words truly understood how awestruck they should have been in this moment. Jesus told them that His followers would be able to know Him as intimately as He knows and is known by the Father. How can this possibly be?

The answer is found at the core of why Jesus came. Christ ultimately came to solve humanity's greatest crisis. This was an epidemic that humanity had no hope of rectifying itself. Humanity found itself at the crossroads of sin's peril, shackled to its wages and penalty of death. Christ came to restore that which was broken by literally becoming sin so that humanity's debt could be paid in full, and our relationship with the Father could be completely and definitively restored.

His purpose and mission, rooted in love, could be summarized in one word: Relationship.

What is paramount in every healthy relationship? Communication. This is why in Jesus' very next breath he said, *"I have other sheep, which are not of this fold; I must bring them also, and They will hear My voice, and they will become one flock with one shepherd."* (John 10:16)

This brings us to a pivotal question. Do you hear the voice of your shepherd? If not, it's time to draw near. Jesus did not give his life to restore a relationship with you just to give you the cold shoulder. The truth is, He is constantly speaking, revealing more of Himself and more of who you really are and the purposes and plans He has for you. Throughout Jesus' life, we know that everything He did, He did because it was what He saw and heard His father doing. John 10 makes it crystal clear that the same level of intimacy is available to each of us.

I cannot tell you how excited I am that you are holding this book in your hands. I believe that this is by no means a coincidence. I believe this is a "Holy Spirit set-up," a divine appointment set by the Father to help show you that you too can have "ears to hear," as the Father is longing to speak life into you.

Over the past 20 years that I have been blessed to know Penny Renfroe, I have been blown away by her passion to hear what the Spirit of God is wanting to say RIGHT NOW and her sensitivity to His voice. I am also encouraged and inspired by her passion to help other people know that God is speaking to them and that they, too, can be hearers of His ruach word, His Spirit-breathed word.

In the pages that follow, you are going to get a glimpse into her prayer closet, a place that she frequents in order to hear His still small voice and His holy roar. I pray that as you navigate the pages to come, you too will sense the grace and mercy and love of the Father and His desire for you to more fully know and experience Him. He is ready to reveal Himself to you. Are you ready?

Will Rupert
Pastor, OneChurch Whitesboro
Whitesboro, Texas

Preface

The beauty in relationship is communication. As a Believer in Jesus, it is my belief that I have an intimate relationship with Him as not only my savior, but also my Lord. I believe that anyone who trusts in the resurrected Christ has access to this personal relationship. I share the steps to beginning this relationship in the closing notes of this book, so that anyone seeking to enter into this relationship with Jesus may do so today!

In my younger years, when it came to communicating with God, I did all the talking and not much listening. I lacked the discernment of His voice. I intensely desired to hear Him, but I didn't believe that I had "ears to hear."

When I grew in intimacy with God, I began to recognize Him speaking to me. I know that He was always speaking to me; it's His very nature. He is The Word! The more I distinguished His voice, the more adept I became at tuning in to it.

In true conversational form, this book includes both my words and those of the Father. To appreciate the ebb and flow of exchange, some entries are shorter, and some are longer. This is the reality of my fellowship with Him. Just as in my interactions with Him, some entries conclude with a prayer, and some do not. In an effort to be transparent, for the most part, I have left entries just as they came to me.

In some cases, I have included details of dreams or pictures that I had. From those visions, the Holy Spirit will elaborate on their significance or, as I like to say, "unpack" their meaning for me and bring revelation through them. Previously, in my quest to learn, there were many times I heard someone share only the "what," but not the "how" of God speaking to them (the vision or dream or word). When I only heard the "what," it often left me confused and believing that I could never hear God because I did not understand the "how." I find it encouraging for others who are desiring to more effectively distinguish the voice of the Lord when they realize they are hearing God in many of the same ways that I do.

Often the Father speaks to me in an allegory. I like to say, "The 'thing' is not the 'thing,' but represents the 'thing.'" It is like the parables that Jesus taught in the Bible. When the reader finds this symbolic language, look for the underlying meanings and allow Holy Spirit to bring individual revelation specific to him.

In order that the reader may readily grasp the source, whether it be in my voice or Holy Spirit's, I have included a visual indication with each entry. The needle and thread image on the pages that follow indicate the Lord has authored the message to me, or to you, through the writing.

Join me in the conversation as we experience Him together.

Acknowledgements

I must begin by thanking my husband, Rusty, for his patience and support over the years while I spent time with a journal or, more recently, a laptop. Rusty, thank you for honoring the call that God has on my life and for serving alongside me. Your love means the world to me!

To my children, Reagan and Jordan, and my daughter-in-love, Jonnah, I love you with my whole heart! And to my photographer, Reagan, thank you so much for your time and patience with me!

Two of my father's sisters, Sandy Plummer and Sue Hanning, have been cheerleaders for me as long as I've been alive. Over the past several years, they have encouraged me right into this process! Thank you both for believing in me!

To my friends, Eric and Sandy Keller, I appreciate you! You have inspired me, walked with me through this process, proofread for me, and rallied around me. Bless ya!

To my friend Jamie Wisener, I am so grateful for all your help! You're the best!

To my besties, Dana, Kim, and Sandy, I love ya!

To the Renfroe BeGroup, I love and value you all! You have prayed for us and prophesied over us and believed for us from day one! We couldn't have asked for more grace-filled people to do life with. Thank you, Hayes's, Hendersons, Kellers, Ms. Lynne, Stokes, Val, and Woods!

To OneChurch Whitesboro, I say a most sincere "Thank you!" You are the body of Christ to us, and we love you all and thank God for planting us with you! To each one of my Deeper crew that said, "Write the book," thank you!

To my pastor and beloved friend, Will Rupert, thank you for giving me space to walk in my calling! I will forever thank God for knitting our hearts with yours!

This project began with the best coach, Jill Hellwig and Brand New U. Jill, I absolutely could not have imagined how incredible this experience would be. Thank you for pushing, pulling, and getting the best of all I had to give! You are a gift!

To my patient publisher, Mary Ethel Eckard, thank you for allowing me to go at my own pace! You took years of journal entries and turned them into a beautiful tapestry of the Father's for His Glory! What a treasured skill for His Kingdom!

To my new friend and lead marketer, Lisa Williams, I still don't know how you did all you've done! You took my meager meanderings and turned them into words that people could connect and understand. Thank you!

To my parents Steve and Glenda Culpepper, who dance with Jesus today, I express my sincerest gratitude for a legacy of faith. What you imparted to me is beyond measure, and I cannot thank God enough for a lifetime of love and sacrifice that you modeled for me. I love you!

To my Jesus, how can I ever express my gratitude that You would choose to reveal Yourself to me. I live to hear Your voice and to experience Your presence. May I always walk in step with you, Holy Spirit, and show a desperate world that they, too, can live in true relationship with You!

Penny

Introduction

In April of 2009, I wrote in my journal, "I want to know the mysteries of God!" In 2015, I realized that God speaks to me and through me when I write. In the years since, I have penned His words and revelations in my journals as an encouragement and reminder of His love, leading, revelations, and wisdom. Over the past few years, I began to sense that He wanted me to share these writings with others. When I questioned how I was to string these writings together, so they made sense, He responded as follows:

"Penny, you are a weaver, a bobbin worker. Each of my people is a unique thread, created especially for the assignment they have been given to carry out. Their beauty and their various hues of color blend perfectly with the fabric of their lives. In those who trust Me, I am the bottom thread, the stabilizing endowment in their lives. I join with them to lock each stitch into place. I'm not seen on the presentation of the fabric, but I am intricately wound into each pattern. I'll rise from below and connect with my people to create a sturdy foundation to display the embellishment of my beautiful design.

"Penny, you are the weaver. You are charged with a mission to pull up the threads of My presence and My empowering grace and connect them with the beautiful thread of My peoples' lives, assisting to bridge us together. When I join with an individual, our two threads create a stitching that is secure and held in place. Without the thread of My presence, their thread, their lives, though beautiful and crafted for greatness, are unsecured, vulnerable, and not likely to hold their position. I am crucial to the stability and longevity of the project.

"Know your role, and what your role is not. You are not the top thread. Do not superimpose your desires over the lives of others.

"You are not the bottom thread. I AM.

"You are not the answer to others' problems or dilemmas. You don't have the power, nor the expertise, to fix them. You just point them to Me.

"You are not the power operating the machine. No amount of striving on your part can adequately produce the results that I can through My grace.

"Yours is to partner with Me, to showcase My living Word, to create an opportunity for others to recognize Me at work in their worlds, and to enable an open door and network for them to work with Me."

The common thread in each of these writings is His faithfulness. I pray you will be blessed as you allow Him to weave each thread within this book into the tapestry of your life, to draw nearer to Him, and to become more like Him.

1

The Father's Heart

With pen in hand I wait,
In silence I sit still
Trusting with all confidence
Your heart will be revealed.

I long for words to flow
Straight from Your throne to me,
Bringing grace to life,
And setting my soul free.

New freedom comes through message
From Father's heart so clear.
It sparks a brand new fire
And drives away my fear.

Your words have power and effect,
Not merely men's repeat,
Changing the course of history:
Satan's final defeat.

Like creation's first encounter
With Your voice to bring forth light,
I look with anticipation to note
Fresh revealing of sight.

I tune into Your presence
Like a radio of old,
Cutting through the static
To find your love so bold.

I receive Your thoughts of mercies
And the words You've sent today.
I hide them deep inside myself,
A guide to know Your ways.

Tomorrow I'll be back again
For Your words sustain my being.
To know Your loving kindness
Gives my life true meaning.

2

One With Him

"I continually see the Lord in front of me."
Acts 2:25 b TPT

Acts 2:25 quotes Psalms 16:8 saying, *"For David says of Him, 'I saw the Lord always in my presence; for He is at my right hand, so that I will not be shaken.'"* Another way of saying this is, "I am always beholding the Lord in my presence." This grabbed me by the heart. As a Christian, I know that the Father and I are one and that the Holy Spirit is inside me. I am the house of Holy Spirit. Because He resides in me, He is always in my presence, and I am in His presence.

It is easy, because I know He is always with me, to become complacent about His presence and to take for granted that He is there, to sense Him beside me, and, even in gratitude, not focus on Him. I can be aware of His presence without beholding Him.

My husband and I can be in the same room together and still ignore one another. But when we put aside our other activities, turn off the television or put down the book, and focus our attention fully on one another, our level of intimacy goes up.

This principle is true with God, and David goes on to say, *"Because He is at my right hand, I will not be shaken."*

How many times has God longed to still the shaking in my life, and He would have done so had I chosen to behold Him in my presence.

Turn your eyes upon Jesus
look full in His wonderful face
and the things of earth will grow strangely dim
in the light of His glory and grace.[1]

*"'You will seek Me and find Me when you search for Me with all your heart.
I will be found by you,' declares the Lord,"*
Jeremiah 29:13-14a

*"You draw near to those who call out to you, listening closely,
especially when their hearts are true."*
Psalms 145:18 TPT

3

Turning Toward You

Ow I long for intimacy with you. I am the God of the universe, creator of all things. I don't need anything from you, but I delight in you.

I take great joy in your smile. Oh, how I enjoy time with you when your focus is solely on Me. It is My pleasure to come alongside you and to whisper My love to you. I keep My eye on you, and I'm your biggest cheerleader! Do you hear Me encouraging you?

I'm not keeping score in some grand game. I just want to be with you. And when you give Me your worship, it fills My heart.

I see you, even when you're distracted, even in discouragement and frustration. Please don't turn your face from Me because you think you're lacking or because you feel slighted by circumstances.

I'll not turn from you!

"Draw me after you and let us run together...
We will rejoice in you and be glad;
we will extol your love more than wine. Rightly do they love you."
Song of Solomon 1:4

"For the Lord your God is living among you.
He is a mighty savior.
He will take delight in you with gladness.
With his love, he will calm all your fears.
He will rejoice over you with joyful songs."
Zephaniah 3:17 NLT

4

The Product of Belief

In Judges 13, there is a story about a husband, a wife, and an angel. The angel appeared to the wife (who had been barren) and told her that she would have a son who would deliver their country from its oppressors. The angel gave her some instruction on how to proceed in the pregnancy and how to raise the son.

After she told her husband about this visit from the angel, her husband asked the Lord to send the angel back so he could talk to him. When the angel returned, the husband's first question of him was "What will my son do for a living?"

They had access to all wisdom of God's holy messenger, and he asked, "what will he do?" It is most interesting that the angel did not answer his question but reminded the woman of his previous instruction.

The dad's question from over 3,000 years in history is the same as many of us today. Instead of asking "who will he be?" he asked, "what will he do?"

We are called human beings – not human doings. However, we get caught up in *do this* and d*on't do that* from a list of rules instead of focusing on who we are.

Jesus calls us into a relationship with Him. When we enter that relationship, we call that salvation. It's acknowledging that we are *without* access to God because we are born into a fallen and broken world. We are *without* the resource within ourselves to connect to a perfect God. We are *without* the power to change ourselves.

Then in that relationship with Jesus, we find our real identity. In our house we say, it is "who you *be*" that matters. It's not that what we do doesn't matter; it does. But what we do comes out of what we believe about "who you *be.*" What we truly believe leads to what we do.

For example, I can say I trust God as my provider, but if I'm not generous when he tells me to give to someone, then I don't really believe God will take care of my own needs; I am operating from an I-don't-have-enough mentality.

When Satan tempted Eve in the Garden of Eden (Genesis 3), he went after what she believed. She began to doubt what she believed about God and bought the lie that He was holding out on them. When she ate of the forbidden fruit, it was the result of her unbelief. Her behavior was the product of her belief.

"God saved you by his grace when you believed.
And you can't take credit for this;
it is a gift from God. Salvation is not a reward
for the good things we have done,
so none of us can boast about it. For we are God's
masterpiece. He has created us anew
in Christ Jesus, so we can do the good things he planned for us long ago."
Ephesians 2:8-10 NLT

"Jesus answered, 'The work you can do for God starts
with believing in the One he has sent.'"
John 6:29 TPT

"...that if you confess with your mouth Jesus
as Lord, and believe in your heart
that God raised Him from the dead, you will be saved."
Romans 10:9

5

Cadence

Lord, I perpetually listen for the sound of cadence. There are times that I receive my marching orders from You, and I join in step, right into formation, into the place You've kept for me.

There are other times I wait for the orders; I listen for the cadence. In anticipating the command, I miss the opportunity for rest. In the time that You've set aside for recovery and sustenance and rejuvenation, I am so tense with anticipation, I don't receive what is here for me.

There is tension between being "at the ready" for my coming assignment and spending all my time at a closed gate to the exclusion of today's provision. *"You prepare a table before me in the presence of my enemies"* (Psalms 23:5a AMP). You desire that I sit and eat – not bypass the nutrition in order to jump up and down and wave my sword in the face of the enemy.

Today may I rest at the table of Your abundance, relishing the meats and the delicacies that will strengthen and fortify me. Because my attention is trained on Your holy face, I'll not miss Your wink of favor toward me, nor Your change of expression that prepares me to look forward to the gate. I will receive all You have for me here, and when I get the nod, I'll step into my place to partner with You in the assignment.

> Jesus,
>
> You are my Sabbath rest! I will rest in Your finished work and take respite as You refill my soul and replenish my supply before my next assignment. I choose to pause and take delight in You.
>
> Amen

"You become my delicious feast
even when my enemies dare to fight.
You anoint me with the fragrance of your Holy Spirit;
you give me all I can drink of you until my cup overflows."
Psalms 23:5 TPT

"So there is a special rest still waiting for the people of God.[2]
For all who have entered into God's rest have rested from their labors,
just as God did after creating the world."
Hebrews 4:9-10 NLT

6

Pursue Me

I'm not hiding from you. You look from side to side, catching glimpses of Me. Like a passing vapor, you notice, but then it quickly dissipates.

It's not that I'm playing hide and seek with you. I don't run when I know you're looking for Me.

I give You these glimpses so that you'll recognize Me and pursue My presence. I am lovingly enticing you, calling out to you to get your attention, hoping that you'll seek Me with unbridled passion. With singular focus, I want you to enter My abode knowing that I am good. Be ready to receive My goodness and all that I have for you.

I am here for you to experience My love and justice and grace and mercy. I will pour it all out for you and in you anew.

When you sense My nearness, pause and look deeper. I long to be found by You!

"What bliss you experience when your heart is pure!
For then your eyes will open to see more and more of God."
Matthew 5:8 TPT

"Stick close to my instruction, my son,
and follow all my advice."
Proverbs 7:1 TPT

7

Hearing His Voice

"Solid food is for the mature, whose spiritual senses perceive heavenly matters. And they have been adequately trained by what they've experienced to emerge with understanding of the difference between what is truly excellent and what is evil and harmful."
Hebrews 5:14 TPT

We train our senses by constant use. It is by reason of use and practice that we gain discernment and distinguish the voice of God.

I heard the Lord speak to me. It is absolutely incredible that the God of the universe desires to talk to me personally. I am still learning to distinguish His voice, knowing that it sounds just like mine in my head. What He said was so true, but so humbling. "You want to hear, but you don't want to listen."

When my daughter was about six years old, she said, "Mom, I asked Jesus a question, and I really want to know the answer, but I can't quit talking in my head!" Wow! Oh, Sweetie, I have the same problem! That memory is as vivid as it if happened yesterday. And here I am over 20 years later and still having the same struggle: to stop talking in my head!

I have found myself at times begging to hear the voice of God, while knowing full well that He is always speaking. It is my hearer that has been plugged by distraction, noise, and talking in my head! God doesn't want to shout at me, but I'm not quiet long enough to practice listening.

Then comes the question, "Okay, so what are you going to do with this revelation? How much do you really want to hear? I don't speak sporadically but want to communicate with you all day about the smallest of details, because I care about your life."

I am intentionally listening to hear even the smallest of details, because in hearing even the slightest message, I practice. Like an old-fashioned radio, I am tuning my ear from the static and extraneous buzzing to hone-in on His voice. I'm exercising and training my senses to recognize His voice.

By reason of use, I will gain discernment to hear the very voice of God.

"Ask me and I will tell you remarkable secrets you
do not know about things to come."
Jeremiah 33:3 NLT

"Heaven and earth will pass away, but My words will not pass away."
Matthew 24:35

"God, all at once you turned on a floodlight for me!
You are the revelation-light in my darkness,
and in your brightness I can see the path ahead."
Psalms 18:28 TPT

8

You are on a precipice. When I revealed that message to you, your natural imagination took you to a dry desert place of giant red rocks. You saw yourself standing on the edge of an unknown with trepidation about being expected to take a giant leap into an unknown void, struggling to find your footing and the next platform from which to operate.

But that is not the precipice I have you on in this season. Instead, you are on the crest. You've been navigating your way through deep waters, and the waves of My presence are building. You're now riding a giant swell, and you can trust that I am directing and governing the divine movement.

The upsurge is now crescendoing into a holy break. That's where you find yourself in this season. You've experienced an intensification of both My anointing and My assignment. You are about to experience a culmination in this time that will present as elevation and a new outlook from the pinnacle of the breaker.

Soon I will prompt you to make the jump at the opportune time. I'm creating the perfect wave for you to ride. As you move from the apex to enter the tube of my covering, you will be filled with the joy of adventure and the peace of knowing that you're gliding in My provision.

Don't be so consumed with the coming ride that you miss the vision and perspective that I'm unveiling for you in this time. Don't jump prematurely or you'll find yourself on a shorter excursion than I have prepared for you. But don't delay when you hear My perfectly timed directive: "Now!"

You'll drop in to a specially formed barrel that will provide a glassy smooth view. There will be times that you must adjust your stance as you maneuver through the wave's push and pull, but as you respond to My voice, I will establish your footing.

Prepare your heart. Practice listening for My direction. Look for My hand as it forms your future opportunities. Believe with Me. Agree with My word. And respond quickly when I move you. You're in for the greatest ride of your life!

"'Not by might, nor by power, but by My Spirit [of whom
the oil is a symbol],' *says the Lord of hosts."*
Zechariah 4:6 b AMP

"O my dove, in the clefts of the rock, in the secret place of the steep pathway,
let me see your form, let me hear your voice;
for your voice is sweet, and your form is lovely."
Song of Solomon 2:14

9

Next

Sometimes God will persistently leave us in a circumstance until we make the decision to get our hearts right. This is because He knows there is no space for what we are carrying in our "next."

Getting our heart right can look like letting go of offense. When we move forward with that same chip on our shoulder, we will just be looking for reasons to validate its existence. We will find what we are looking for, one way or another.

It can look like forgiveness. When we move into the next season with unforgiveness, it is like asking to receive with a closed fist. When we forgive and release someone from "owing us," it's like opening our hands to the Father, and He will fill them with blessing.

It can also look like giving ourselves relief from frustration over unfulfilled dreams or expectations. Let us hold fast to the promises of God and partner with Him in anticipation of seeing His word come to pass. But let's let go of the resentment because we have not seen what we expected, either from God or from others or from ourselves.

The situation can also look like moving past regret over failures or missteps. Of course, we will make mistakes because we are race of people born into a fallen world, and when we put our faith and trust and hope in Jesus, we experience His full forgiveness, and our spirit (the real us) is reborn. But even as we walk out this new creation (2 Corinthians 5:17), we still stumble.

As believers in Jesus, we acknowledge our faults to Him (because it cleanses our conscience) and we receive His healing. *"But there is now no more condemnation for those who are in Christ Jesus"* (Romans 8:1). If we have trusted Jesus, we are forgiven; it is finished. He is not condemning us.

But we often cannot seem to forgive ourselves. When we carry that guilt and shame and denigration, it becomes a heavy burden, assaulting us from within. Receive forgiveness, make amends if Holy Spirit directs, and then unlock the self-imposed chains of accusation and lamenting. Going forward think differently, believe differently, and do differently.

Some of us need to let go of faulty belief systems. We have incorrect doctrines and wrong thinking. It may be that in the next season, we need the revelation of the goodness of God in order to be and do what He's calling forth in us. Perhaps we need a repentance in our thinking to realize that God is speaking, and we can hear. I may have a faulty belief system that God is the source of the bad thing that is happening to me; if that is the case, I will never fully trust Him to bring me through it.

Once we loose the things binding us in our present, we will have the freedom and the unleashing to move forward. We often step into something new in the same way we left the something old. Let us move out of the present season with gratitude for what we have received and learned, mercy for others, grace for ourselves, and a resolve to keep our hands and hearts open to what God wants to do in the new!

"Not that I have already obtained it [this goal of being Christlike]
or have already been made perfect, but I actively press on
so that I may take hold of that [perfection] *for*
which Christ Jesus took hold of me
and made me His own. I press on toward the goal to win the [heavenly] *prize*
of the upward call of God in Christ Jesus."
Philippians 3:12, 14 AMP

"But this I call to mind, Therefore I have hope. It is
because of the Lord's loving kindnesses
that we are not consumed, Because His [tender] *compassions never fail.*
They are new every morning; Great and beyond measure is Your faithfulness.

*'The Lord is my portion and my inheritance,' says
my soul; 'Therefore I have hope in Him
and wait expectantly for Him.' The Lord is good to
those who wait* [confidently] *for Him,
To those who seek Him* [on the authority of God's word]."
Lamentations 3:21-25 AMP

*"Instead fully immerse yourselves into the Lord Jesus, the Anointed One,
and don't waste even a moment's thought on your
former identity to awaken its selfish desires."*
Romans 13:14 TPT

10

Sometimes you're so eager for a product that you try to *produce* the first thing you see. Not that what you see isn't valid, because it is. And I'll never *waste* a Word that I've spoken to you.

But be patient. Don't take off running with the first hint of My presence and turn it into a product so you can check your spiritual box. Oh, how far you've come in hearing and distinguishing My voice over the past seasons.

But intimacy with Me isn't a product to display. It's a process to be lived and shared. I'm not saying that our relationship is not to be shared as a way to encourage others. What I am saying is that sometimes you hear, transcribe, and then stop listening for more. I desire to keep downloading, but you're stopping short.

The first word isn't the last word. Keep listening; there's more: more revelation, more layers, more insight, more depth, and more love and grace that I long to pour into you.

My presence has to be enough. My Word is eternal and is without fail. My promises are yes and amen. My voice is resounding, and the world is held in place by the power of My spoken Word. Don't spend energy chasing these attributes of Me and bypass My presence for sparkly and shiny eye-catchers. Let My Spirit reveal truth and enable you to walk in My complete love.

God,

I don't want to produce a product. I want to share My life with You and use what You pour into me to lift up others. Thank You for speaking to me, for me, and for others that I might build up the Body of Christ.

Amen

"The unfolding of Your words gives light; it gives understanding to the simple."
Psalms 119:130

"Deep calls to deep at the sound of Your waterfalls; all Your breakers and Your waves have rolled over me."
Psalms 42:7

11

Forevermore

I hear a rumbling in the distance. I suspect that rain is coming. I can smell its sweet scent in the air, and the breeze has just brought a cool touch in its spring warmth.

There are rumblings in the Spirit as well. Growing stronger and more frequent, the sound of His voice is coming with clarity and power.

Just as lightning strikes its target and the sound of thunder follows, God is pulling back His bow and sending His Word like a piercing arrow directly to its intended target. That arrow is not for our demise, rather to bring instruction and a message of life.

As the coming clouds release their storehouse of rain on us, we reap the benefit of their blessing. The sweetness of the spring shower falls on us like a fresh anointing.

His Word falls on us and surrounds us with presence and joy. His words are life and peace. We drink them in, and we are nourished, refreshed, renewed, and rejuvenated. His arrow has met its target: life forevermore.

> *"Those who trust in and rely on the Lord* [with confident expectation] *are like Mount Zion, which cannot be moved but remains forever. As the mountains surround Jerusalem, so the Lord surrounds His people from this time forth and forever."*
> Psalms 125:1-2 AMP

*"He answered, 'The Scriptures say: Bread alone will not satisfy,
but true life is found in every word that constantly
goes forth from God's mouth.'"*
Matthew 4:4 TPT

*"But what does it say? 'The word is near you,
in your mouth and in your heart'
—that is, the word* [the message, the basis] *of faith which we preach."*
Romans 10:8 AMP

12

I see you opening the door where you live. The atmosphere is different out here. You feel you're not ready to step completely outside and into a new way of doing life. I understand your hesitation, and I love that you are looking in My direction and seeking Me.

I celebrate that you've opened the door a crack, and My breeze, My breath, My presence are entering your abode and bringing a fresh sense of renewal. As you experience Me more and more, you'll find yourself opening the door a little further to allow Me access to more of you. One day, you will look up and declare, "Swing wide the gate!" You will relish the communion with Me as you experience the fullness of My love.

Then, you will step outside your doors, in a bold step of faith and trust, into My wide-open vastness. Here I will show you new things and will reveal mysteries of My kingdom to you.

I invite you to be vulnerable – not so that I may take advantage of you, but so that I can impart more of Myself to you.

Today I rejoice that you've opened the door! Relax and enjoy My companionship. As you go about your day, speak to Me, and listen for My voice. You are the apple of My eye. I can't wait to BE with you!

"Behold, I stand at the door and knock; if anyone hears My voice and opens the door, I will come in to him and will dine with him, and he with Me."
Revelation 3:20

*"Come to Me all you who are weary and heavy
laden, and I will give you rest!"*
Matthew 11:28

13

Control the Flow

I see a stone wall and at the top of the wall there are openings for water to flow. When I look, I see only a small sprinkling from the source going down the wall. It's nice, and it looks refreshing, and I imagine it could be cooling, and the sound could be relaxing. But immediately I know that it's only a small portion of what is available and possible. It could be minimally satisfying, but its potential to be sustaining is in question.

God says, "You control the flow."

We can meander over and get a taste of His goodness, or we can open the well of His living water and begin to drink it in! He has given us all of Himself in Messiah; He isn't withholding any good thing from us.

We should become so enamored in the presence of the Father that we carry the residue of being with Him to a world desperate to experience the color and magnificence of His glory.

Turn up the dial on His supply and let the Father lavish Himself onto you.

"In the days of desert dryness, he split open the mighty rock,
and the waters flowed like a river before their very eyes.
He gave them all they wanted to drink from his living springs."
Psalms 78:15-16 TPT

"O God of my life, I'm lovesick for you in this weary wilderness.
I thirst with the deepest longings to love you more,
with cravings in my heart that can't be described.
Such yearning grips my soul for you, my God!"
Psalms 63:1 TPT

14

Speak, Lord

When I sit in Your presence, my senses are piqued. My appetite is whetted for a coming message. I'm intrigued and roused from my common mental meanderings to a place of anticipation. My mind is awakened in sharp form to hone in on detail and the mere nuances of the surrounding opportunities.

Jesus, wrap your arms around me like holy bubble wrap. Fill each compartment with Your very breath. Surround me with Your song of comfort that brings peace that I can't contain.

When You fill my every space with Your presence, there's nothing left of me but a reflection of You. Let Your mercy rush in and blow like a warm breath on my face that's turned toward You.

Speak, Lord, for Your servant is listening.

"Truth's shining light guides me in my choices and decisions;
the revelation of your Word makes my pathway clear."
Psalms 119:105 TPT

"But from there you will seek the Lord your God, and you will find Him
if you search for Him with all your heart and all your soul. When you
are in distress and all these things have come upon you, in the latter days
you will return to the Lord your God and listen to His voice. For the Lord
your God is a compassionate God; He will not fail you nor destroy you
nor forget the covenant with your fathers which He swore to them."
Deuteronomy 4:29-31

15

Garment of Praise

In a dream, I was at a house with several other women (unknown) and a young groom brought his bride to us to *"get her ready"* for the wedding ceremony. She was very young and quiet, reserved. We brought her into a room and began. He then came to the door of the room carrying a wedding gown in a plastic covering. He said, "This is the dress," and gave it to me. That was the only specific instruction he gave me.

We went into the room and proceeded to do her hair and make-up. She put on a dress, and as we were doing the finishing touches, I realized she was wearing the wrong dress. We hadn't put on the dress that the groom had brought to me. We quickly brought out the correct dress and changed her into it. I thought, "Oh dear, I almost didn't do the one thing he asked me to!"

In my haste to get her ready, I had not put on my own make-up, and I, too, was wearing the wrong dress. (I was to be a bridesmaid and I wasn't in my bridesmaid's dress.). I quickly changed my dress and spent the rest of the dream trying to finish getting "ready."

The groom in this dream is a representation of Jesus. His young bride is the Church. He brought her to us to "make ready." The dress he brought to me was a garment. It was my only specific instruction. In my haste to do my assignment, I had not put on my own garment. When the revelation of this dream began to unfold, and I connected the garment to the dress, I immediately thought of the phrase, "garment of praise."

Praise opens the door of our own hearts. With Jesus as our Redeemer, we now have access to the Father. We have become so focused on the outside adorning (hair and make-up) behaviors and good deeds, making things look good, that we have stopped prioritizing the garments Jesus gave us and told us to wear. Put on the garment of praise and it will overtake the spirit of heaviness. We don't first battle the spirit of heaviness so that we can wear the garment of praise. We put on the garment of praise, regardless of our circumstances and feelings, and that garment has the power to change our soul (mind, will, and emotions).

"The Spirit of the Lord God is upon me, because the Lord has anointed
and commissioned me … to grant to those who mourn in Zion the following:
to give them a turban instead of dust [on their heads a sign of mourning],
the oil of joy instead of mourning,
the garment [expressive] of praise instead of a disheartened spirit.
So they will be called trees of righteousness
[strong and magnificent, distinguished for integrity,
justice, and right standing with God],
the planting of the Lord, that He may be glorified."
Isaiah 61:1a, 3 AMP

"Be in awe before His majesty. Be in awe before such power and might!
Come worship wonderful Yahweh, arrayed in all His splendor,
bowing in worship as He appears in the beauty of holiness.
Give Him the honor due His name. Worship Him wearing
the glory-garments of your holy, priestly calling."
Psalms 29:2 TPT 15

16

Intimacy

O h, My goodness, Daughter! How I love you. There has not been a day in your walk on earth that I haven't loved you, pursued your heart, and walked alongside you.

There have been dark days and lonely nights when I knelt beside your bed and stroked your hair as you tossed and turned and longed for comfort. No matter how you felt along the way during those moments, My presence and My comfort were there for you.

Even now, I long to pour out My peace on you, like oil on your head. Receive it all. Open your heart and let Me fill you! Again, and again, and again!

I have a depth of intimacy for which you've only wished. You've not had the courage to even speak your desire to Me. It's an unspoken longing that sits just beneath the surface of your life. You consider it lightly, and casually wish that our relationship was different. You go about your life, and you're satisfied, but I'm about to make your longing a reality.

This is real.
You can trust Me.
It can be different than what you've experienced.
Lean into Me.

"You will make known to me the path of life;
in Your presence is fullness of joy;
In Your right hand there are pleasures forever."
Psalms 16:11

"When Yahweh delights in how you live your life,
he establishes your every step.
If they stumble badly they will still survive,
for the Lord lifts them up with his hands.
I was once inexperienced, but now I'm old.
Not once have I found a lover of God forsaken by him,
nor have any of their children gone hungry."
Psalms 37:23-25 TPT

17

Yield

Why is it that at the first hint of conflict, my stomach churns? I long to stand still and see the salvation of my God. Mostly the salvation part, but I would love to be able to be calm in the stand still part.

When I see the seeming insanity of this world, my mind immediately begins to rationalize a worthy argument. My personality tries to transcend the crazy and asserts the belief that if I could just make "them" understand, "they" would come out from the fog of unbelief, dysfunction, and wackiness to see the light.

But ultimately, all the persuasion in my wheelhouse won't transform a mind. I can offer understanding and insight into truth (real truth), but it is up to every individual to submit his own will to receive what God has for him. It is up to Holy Spirit to draw men to Jesus, to reveal all truth, and to bring about lasting change.

I can be empowered by Holy Spirit with words of knowledge, words of wisdom, dreams and visions of insight, but it is only by someone's yielding that they can fully receive what God wants to give. So now, I stand still, I wait, and I will see the salvation of my God.

> *"God, the searcher of the heart, knows fully our longings,*
> *yet he also understands the desires of the Spirit,*
> *because the Holy Spirit passionately pleads before God for us,*
> *his holy ones, in perfect harmony with God's plan and our destiny."*
> Romans 8:27 TPT

"Answer me when I call to you,
O God who declares me innocent.
Free me from my troubles.
Have mercy on me and hear my prayer."
Psalms 4:1 NLT

18

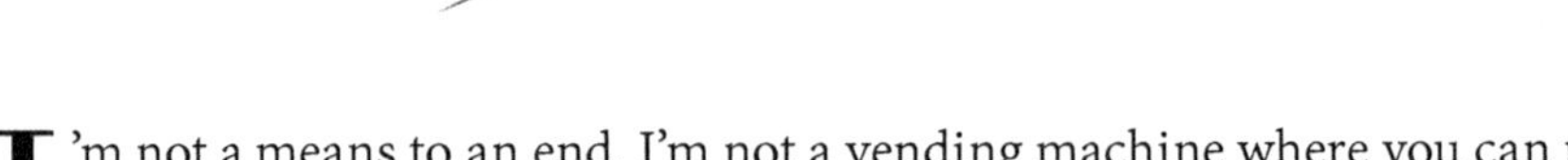

I'm not a means to an end. I'm not a vending machine where you can pay a token and receive a blessing.

I am God of the universe, and I have all things at my disposal. I'm not limited to dishing out what will conveniently fit into your container. I have more for you than you can comprehend, but it's not dependent on your tokens.

Come to Me out of relationship and love for Me. Even there, I'll supply you with all you need. I'll pour Myself out from the well of My presence.

As you draw near, you'll experience My manifest presence in new and fresh ways that are more than mere blessings. The intimacy you experience with Me will give you strength, direction, and a sustaining joy. Put away your tokens and come walk with Me!

"Trust in the Lord completely, and do not rely on your own
opinions. With all your heart rely on him to guide you, and he will
lead you in every decision you make. Become intimate with him
in whatever you do, and he will lead you wherever you go."
Proverbs 3:5-6 TPT

"Come to Me, all who are weary and heavily burdened
[by religious rituals that provide no peace],
and I will give you rest [refreshing your souls with salvation].

Take My yoke upon you and learn from Me [following Me as My disciple],
for I am gentle and humble in heart,
and you will find rest [renewal, blessed quiet] for your souls.
For My yoke is easy [to bear] and My burden is light."
Matthew 11:28-30 AMP

19

Mosaic

Fully surrendered,
Draw me gently;
Sweetly broken,
Pieces strewn on the floor.

How strange that I feel no pain in my brokenness; only peace filling and covering me. I look at these pieces, like little shards of glass with colors of green and blue. With sharp edges, I know they would be dangerous to handle. But You speak and they come into place, forming something new and beautiful out of my brokenness.

Pieces placed with perfection – that's the finished product I see and in which I take joy and pleasure. I take delight in noting how each piece suits its neighbors with perfection, as if they'd been created together. I notice the shiny connections that seem to be without flaw, and I am amazed.

I can't seem to recall the panic I held in my heart as I saw the broken pieces strewn about on the floor. I couldn't imagine that anything beautiful could ever come out of this tragic mess.

As the colors meld together, I catch my breath at the splendor of the deep hues I never thought existed inside me. You take measly pieces and create something new and beautiful. Had I known and appreciated all that was possible, perhaps I would not have fought so hard to hold it all together on my own.

But, Lord, out of Your goodness, You've created a masterpiece, a priceless treasure full of promise, more beautiful than I could have dreamed.

"For we are God's masterpiece. He has created us anew in Christ Jesus,
So we can do the good things he planned for us long ago."
Ephesians 2:10 NLT

"For you formed my inward parts; you wove me in my mother's womb.
I will give thanks to You, for I am fearfully and wonderfully made.
Wonderful are Your works, and my soul knows it very well."
Psalms 139:13-14

20

Beauty for Ashes

In a vision, I saw a pearl on the bed of the ocean. Plants were swaying with the movement of the water. Then I saw the inside of an oyster shell, shiny with pink iridescent colors. It was beautiful, and it held a single large perfect pearl.

The Lord says, "The thing that causes you irritation today I will transform into a beautiful and valuable treasure."

A pearl is formed when an irritant finds its way into an oyster's shell. This is commonly a single grain of sand. Consider the comparison to getting a pebble in your shoe. You can remove the shoe and, thus, the pebble. In contrast, the oyster has no way of removing the invader, but what he can do is nothing short of miraculous.

He emits a fluid that coats the irritant. This extraordinary secretion surrounds the pest to provide relief from its grating presence. As the creature lives and moves in its home, the irritant is rolled and smoothed, but the reprieve from discomfort is short-lived. So the process continues, layer by layer, as the oyster does what he is created to do, until a perfect pearl is formed.

The oyster doesn't strive to construct something. He doesn't strain to release this fascinating substance. He just submits to God's perfect design. Through this process of submission, the oyster bears a precious and rare treasure.

This is the way it is with us. God promises to give us beauty for our ashes. He gives us something beautiful and of great value in our lives when we submit to Him the things that are dead and dirty and smelly. This is not an exchange where we hand Him one thing and He hands us something better; this is a transformation of our yielded troubles and aggravations.

Many times, God is just waiting for us to come to the end of our meager attempts to fix and control things in our flesh (our own hard work and mental manipulations apart from Him). When we finally raise our hands and surrender to Him, we authorize Him to work things out on our behalf. It is then that we can partner with Him to plant the seeds of beauty among our ashes of self-effort. He will release in us and through us a holy revolutionizing process of transformation.

Jesus, lead us today into Your process of transformation. We relinquish our right to control and demand. We give You the ashes of our efforts that have only brought dust and regret. Fashion something exquisite to be used by You for Your kingdom purpose.

"My child, trade your ashes for joy.

"When you submit your ashes (what remains of your sacrifice, the leftovers of your dead works, and the symbol of your suffering), I will use it to nourish the soil of your life. I can supply your ashes with the building blocks of real life as you pour it out on the ground.

"Ashes in a bucket will never produce life - only memories of what was. If you allow Me, I will bring beauty and food and new sustenance for you. It is only when you pour it out that I can work.

"I am going to adorn you with the memorials of my goodness. I will design for you a garland (lei) of my faithfulness and place it over your head (overcoming your mind and thoughts) and put it around your neck as an ornament and reminder to both you and every beholder."

"Again, the kingdom of Heaven is like a merchant on the
lookout for choice pearls. When he discovered a pearl of great
value, he sold everything he owned and bought it!"
Matthew 13:45-46 NLT

"To all who mourn in Israel, he will give [yield or bring forth] a crown of beauty for ashes, a joyous blessing instead of mourning, festive praise instead of despair. In their righteousness, they will be like great oaks that the Lord has planted for his own glory."
Isaiah 61:3 NLT

"...to strengthen those crushed by despair who mourn in Zion —to give them a beautiful bouquet in the places of ashes, the oil of bliss instead of tears, and the mantle of Joyous praise instead of the spirit of heaviness. Because of this, they will be known as mighty oaks of righteousness, planted by Yahweh as a living display of His glory."
Isaiah 61:3 TPT

21

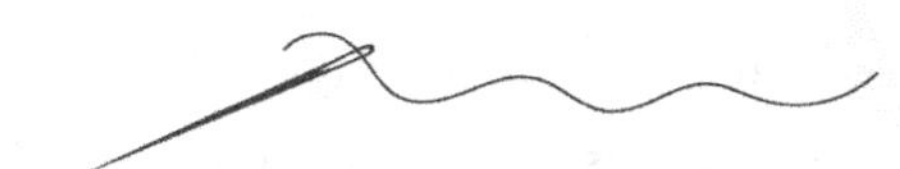

Only I could truly know the cost of the oil in your alabaster box.

I know the cost. I know what it was like when I found you. I've already counted the cost to redeem you and found you worth it. I choose you every time.

I see you. And I saw what life cost you before you turned to Me. I saw your pain, your struggle, the utter frustration. I saw your dreams that lay in a puddle on a dark road. I saw the unmet expectations that broke your heart and left you wondering if you'd ever be home.

Now you've found your home in Me. And the transformation that you are experiencing is beautiful! I receive your worship with open arms, and I delight in you. I know what your praise has cost you, and I receive it with the same weight in which you give it.

Pour yourself out before Me and watch Me refill you to overflowing. I will never leave you wanting.

> *"For you have acquired new creation life which is continually*
> *being renewed into the likeness of the One who created you;*
> *giving you the full revelation of God."*
> Colossians 3:10 TPT

> *"For I consider that the sufferings of this present time are not worthy*
> *to be compared with the glory that is to be revealed to us."*
> Romans 8:18

22

Reduce Pressure

I see an average-size water hose. At one end there is a normal opening for the release of content that has gone through the hose. On the supply side of the hose, there are multiple hoses connected together and in one opening all are pouring into the single hose.

I saw immediately that the hose was under incredible pressure. The fluid from these multiple sources was pouring into the single hose, but it could not possibly contain it or move it fast enough to relieve the load. The only possible solution for strain was on the supply side.

As human beings, especially in a season of unrest, contentious spirits, and fear, we have many sources flowing into our lives. We can recognize the hose of our lives and relate to the multiple sources pushing their way toward us to pour into our lives. We can sense the pressure building at times and know the feeling of the mounting tension as we try to manage the competing, and often-times opposing, forces trying to leverage their way through our hose.

But the only way to reduce the pressure and solve the conundrum of too much for our limited hose is on the supply side.

We must identify the sources that don't belong and cap them, or better yet to cut them off at the head. For believers in Jesus, the best way to do that is to ask Holy Spirit, "Help me cut loose every source except You. Help me to walk with You as my only Source, because You will lead me to real life in the here and now, not just life in heaven."

It is not that we ignore all these other issues and sources. But now we run them through the filter of Holy Spirit, and He provides the perspective, the vision to see the fruit, both good and bad, and the grace to empower us to properly address, limit, and manage the negative sources.

Father, let us identify every source that is trying to gain access to our lives. Let us cut off those that bring death (darkness, negativity, bad fruit) and trust You to enable us to run every source through the filter of Holy Spirit. Help us to reduce the pressure on our hose, our soul (mind, will, and emotions) and walk in freedom to share You and serve You! Amen

"And when He said this, He breathed on them and
said to them, 'Receive the Holy Spirit.'"
John 20:22 AMP

"If we live by the Spirit, let us also walk by the Spirit."
Galatians 5:25

"Do not quench [subdue, or be unresponsive to the
working and guidance of] *the* [Holy] *Spirit."*
1 Thessalonians 5:19 AMP

"He will glorify and honor Me, because He [the Holy Spirit]
will take from what is Mine and will disclose it to you."
John 16:14 AMP 18

23

Take Delight

The fountain of My presence is your delight. It rises up from within you, bringing your full provision. In Me, there is fullness of joy. In Me, there is peace for your weary soul (your mind and your emotions). In Me, there is abundant healing for your body.

You are joined together with Christ. As you live and move and go about, I am literally in you. My Spirit is joined with yours, and I am your full supply. Draw on Me.

If you are thirsty, you can go to the faucet in your home and get a drink. But the knowledge of the water's availability won't satisfy you. You must open the tap and drink.

So it is with Me. Recognizing that I'm fully available to you is encouraging and empowering. But when you open and release the valve of My presence and allow Me to fill your life, you'll see change; you'll experience the tangible difference that I can bring to your circumstances; you'll hear My rhema words for you – My now words, My living, today, words for you.

Protect this presence. Place value on it. This prize mystery of Me in you is abundant life.

"May we be one just as the Father and I are one."
John 17:21 TPT

"… Christ in you, the hope of Glory."
Colossians 1:27b

24

A Blank Canvas

The Bible reminds us 365 times (one for each day of the year) to fear not. And the Word goes on to encourage us and tells us to encourage one another. We are not meant to live a life of fear and defeat, but one of courage and victory. God declares that he has good plans for us, *"to give you a future and a hope"* (Jeremiah 29:11 NLT). God laid out good things for us to accomplish and designed them perfectly for us. The Apostle Paul directs us, *"Therefore, encourage one another..."* (1 Thessalonians 5:11a)

The word *"encourage"* is the word *"parakaleo"* in the original Greek writing. The literal meaning is *to call near.* I believe it is meant for us to call God near. *"In Your presence there is fullness of joy"* (Psalms 16:11). It is when we call out to Him, and His tangible companionship is right up next to us, that we are encouraged beyond the present circumstances and can be transformed into the persons and for the assignments He has for us.

Even King David (ancient King of Israel) found himself in a cave, his family kidnapped, and his friends turned against him. In this dreadful time in his life, David managed to get through such adversities. *"... But David strengthened himself in the Lord his God"* (1 Samuel 30:6b). The word *"strengthen"* here is originally written in Hebrew. The Hebrew word *"hazaq"* means *to seize* or to *take courage.* David literally made the choice within himself to lean into God and be in courage. This shows us that we can encourage and strengthen ourselves, but in the Lord our God.

In our own challenging circumstances, we can call out to the God of the universe, trust in His Son, and let His presence fill our hearts and minds so that we are comforted, refreshed, built up, sustained, and empowered. May we all find the fortitude within ourselves to stand in courage with God in us and beside us and behind us, propelling us forward.

"Let the peace of Christ [the inner calm of one who walks daily with Him] *be the controlling factor in your hearts* [deciding and settling questions that arise]. *To this peace indeed you were called as members in one body* [of believers]. *And be thankful* [to God always]."
Colossians 3:15 AMP

"Now may the Lord of peace Himself grant you His peace at all times and in every way [that peace and spiritual well-being that comes to those who walk with Him, regardless of life's circumstances]. *The Lord be with you all."*
2 Thessalonians 3:16 AMP

*"Don't be pulled in different directions or worried about a thing.
Be saturated in prayer throughout each day, offering
your faith-filled requests before God
with overflowing gratitude. Tell him every detail of your life,
then God's wonderful peace that transcends human understanding,
will guard your heart and mind through Jesus Christ."*
Philippians 4:6-7 NLT

25

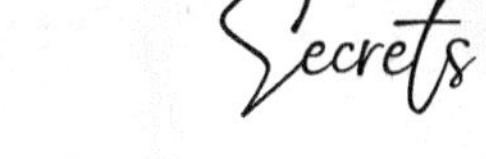

Secrets

My love for you is as sure as the beat of My heart. It is never-ending, timeless, and more certain than the sun. Even when you're not near enough to sense My presence or feel My peace, I'm still there, showering My love on you, around you, and in you.

I've given you the secrets of how to live and be victorious in this temporary life. I know it seems to be confusing when you're in the midst of the noise and chaos. You've developed a picture in your mind of your expectations, then you dismiss those details that don't match your picture.

My plan seldom plays out according to your blueprint and directions. Just because it does not look like you imagined, don't toss it aside without seeking Me and being open to My answer. My thoughts are above yours, so My finished product won't look like your drawing!

Don't ever doubt My incredible love for you but walk in it and see its effects in your life.

I am not limited by your imagination.

I am literally chasing you down with My love. I'm running after you with gifts of grace. My patience is not something you wait on, it's something you live in.

"The secret things belong to the Lord our God,
but the things which are revealed and disclosed
belong to us and to our children forever,
so that we may do all of the words of this law."
Deuteronomy 29:29 AMP

"'Call to Me and I will answer you,
and tell you [and even show you] *great and mighty things,*
[things which have been confined and hidden],
which you do not know and understand and cannot distinguish.'"
Jeremiah 33:3 AMP

26

My Victor

I've been trapped by the strings of religion,
Tethered by my own works,
I've been lured by the promise of freedom
Just to find my state become worse.

I was tricked by the enemy sly.
My single focus became the law,
And soon I was chained and bound.
In looking, I saw only flaws.

Grace rode in on a white horse
In the hand of Jesus my Victor.
There He joined faith and mercy,
My eternal protector.

I'm no longer enslaved to an old law
That Jesus fulfilled in my place.
I now stand redeemed and restored
Thanks to his endless Grace.

In His grace I now find freedom.
In His grace I can see He is light.
Thank You, Jesus my Victor,
You are my life's delight.

27

God With Us

Perhaps you are struggling with something right now and you can't find the answer from God. He has not hidden the answer from you; He has hidden the answer for you. You are not going to get the answer secondhand. You will have to go inside your relationship with Him and seek Him, and He will download it. He has the answer for you. He's hidden it. Dig into the Word and into your relationship with Him. He will reveal it to you.

I see a great canyon with red mountains on every side; the kind where you can see the layers of rock built one upon another over time.

There's a person standing in the bottom of the canyon, looking up and calling out. He's crying out to God and his voice is echoing, reverberating through the canyon. He believes that God will eventually hear him from on high, at the top of the mountain, so he keeps calling and then listening to the sound of his own voice going up and up.

But God says, "Just turn around; I'm right here behind you. You don't have to yell anymore! Turn around and look Me square in the face. I've never left you, and I won't leave you now."

"That is what the Scriptures mean when they say,
'No eye has seen, no ear has heard,
and no mind has imagined
what God has prepared
for those who love him.'
But it was to us that God revealed these things by his Spirit.
For his Spirit searches out everything and shows us God's deep secrets."
1 Corinthians 2:9-10 NLT

*"...that the God of our Lord Jesus Christ, the Father of glory,
may give to you a spirit of wisdom and of revelation in the knowledge of Him.
I pray that the eyes of your heart may be enlightened, so that you will know
what is the hope of His calling, what are the
riches of the glory of His inheritance
in the saints, and what is the surpassing greatness
of His power toward us who believe.
These are in accordance with the working of the strength of His might."*
Ephesians 1:17-19

*"Your own ears will hear him. Right behind you a voice will say,
'This is the way you should go,' whether to the right or to the left."*
Isaiah 30:21 NLT

*"Do not be afraid or discouraged, for the Lord will personally go ahead of you.
He will be with you; he will neither fail you nor abandon you."*
Deuteronomy 31:8 NLT

28

To My Child

In a season of transition, you've found yourself in a period of extended isolation and loneliness. I know your heart, and you've even imagined how this trial would be different if someone were here to weather it with you. It is natural that your fresh wound of loss would appear reopened and particularly raw.

But once again, I want to reach out to you and love you through this time of difficulty and renewed mourning. Even now, those who are on the other side of this thin veil separating us are standing in intercession for you, speaking grace to you.

Don't waver in your faith. I will show Myself strong on your behalf, and I will uphold you with My righteous right hand. I haven't turned away from you. I look squarely at you with eyes full of compassion and mercy, guidance and support. Keep looking for Me and listening for My voice, for My sheep know My voice and won't listen to another. Don't doubt that you are hearing Me! You are!

Stand strong in the power of My might. Lean on me, and I will direct your path.

I love you with an everlasting love; I will build you up again. You'll resume your singing and join in the dance. You'll go back to your work; then you'll sit back and enjoy the fruits of your labor. A harvest of joy is coming for you!

I have told you these things so that My joy and delight may be in you, and that your joy may be full and complete and overflowing.

"Don't be afraid, for I am with you. Don't be discouraged, for I am your God.
I will strengthen you and help you. I will hold you
up with my victorious right hand."
Isaiah 41:10 NLT

"My own sheep will hear my voice and I know each one, and they will
follow me. I give to them the gift of eternal life and they will never be lost
and no one has the power to snatch them out of my hands. My Father, who
has given them to me as his gift, is the mightiest of all, and no one has the
power to snatch them from my Father's care. The Father and I are one."
John 10:27-30 TPT

"A final word: Be strong in the Lord and in his mighty
power. Put on all of God's armor so that you will be able
to stand firm against all strategies of the devil.
For we are not fighting against flesh-and-blood enemies,
but against evil rulers and authorities of the unseen world,
against mighty powers in this dark world, and
against evil spirits in the heavenly places."
Ephesians 6:10-12

29

Anchored

J esus, the very real concerns of this present age are eating away at the soul of Your people. We know Your promises are "Yes and Amen," but there is so much loss, destruction, pain, and suffering.

This is not a new dilemma. There is nothing new under the sun. We can look at times in history that were fraught with troubles where difficulties abounded. In previous years we did not appreciate the time of peace that was upon us. Oh, that season had its challenges, but they seem so much lesser that those of today.

Father, within so much chaos, one word from You can literally transform me.

As I blow from one tent peg to another, I try desperately to grasp something I can anchor onto. I reach out almost without purpose, blindly feeling my way in a dark place.

Suddenly, I feel Your hand catch mine and Your life begins to pulse from Your hand and into my very person. I sense Your power surging throughout my being, but it's not the power or the sensation that brings transformation – it's the Word.

Jesus, the Word, transforms.

Father, give us perspective. Raise our view. Allow us to see with spiritual eyes to distinguish the lies and the ploys of the enemy, and to identify the strategies and assignment that are from You.

"This hope [this confident assurance] *we have as an anchor of the soul* [it cannot slip and it cannot break down under whatever pressure bears

upon it]—a safe and steadfast hope that enters within the veil [of the
heavenly temple, that most Holy Place in which the very presence of God
dwells], *where Jesus has entered [in advance] as a forerunner for us, having
become a High Priest forever according to the order of Melchizedek."*
Hebrews 6:19-20 AMP

"'My thoughts are nothing like your thoughts,' says the Lord.
'And my ways are far beyond anything you could imagine.
For just as the heavens are higher than the earth,
so my ways are higher than your ways
and my thoughts higher than your thoughts.'"
Isaiah 55:8-9 NLT

"Set your mind on the things above, not on the things that are on earth."
Colossians 3:2

*"...while we look not at the things which are seen, but at the
things which are not seen; for the things which are seen are
temporal, but the things which are not seen are eternal."*
2 Corinthians 4:18

30

Harmonies of Life

You were designed for harmony. Your life is a beautiful mixture of notes blending together to create a sound that paints a picture.

This harmony can't be realized in solitude and isolation. Relationships are chords and melodies that come to shape your masterpiece. Community is a beautiful symphony that adds depth and support and creativity in your life.

I do not want you to have twitter relationships. Even My own people have become satisfied with short-term, minimal, and surface-level communication. They choose soundbites that are catchy. They may be truthful, but they aren't leading to deeper and more intimate relationships.

Don't cut yourself off; you would only be limiting the beautiful harmonies in your own life. Come into agreement with Me and then in community to experience the fullness of the sound of My presence and the beauty for your life.

"Therefore encourage one another and build up one another,
just as you also are doing."
1 Thessalonians 5:11

"I urge you, my brothers and sisters, for the sake
of the name of our Lord Jesus Christ,
to agree to live in unity with one another and put to rest
any division that attempts to tear you apart.

31

Sweet Surrender

Planted.

Seed surrendered.

The seed has no expectation of what it is to become. The seed makes no demands on the creator. The seed makes no argument against change. The seed literally dies to itself, in itself.

Through the death of the planted seed, new life emerges. No one mourns the loss of the original seed, just as no one mourns the loss of the caterpillar's form that is sacrificed for the butterfly.

So it should be with you. Planting is painful to the old body, but surrender is sweet when you trust the beauty that is to come.

"Let me make this clear: A single grain of wheat will never
be more than a single grain of wheat unless it drops into the
ground and dies. Because then it sprouts and produces
a great harvest of wheat—all because one grain died."
John 12:24 TPT

"So submit to [the authority of] *God. Resist*
the devil [stand firm against him]
and he will flee from you."
James 4:7 AMP

"O my son, give me your heart. May your eyes
take delight in following my ways."
Proverbs 23:26 NLT

*"Jesus said to all of his followers, 'If you truly desire to be my disciple,
you must disown your life completely, embrace my "cross" as your own,
and surrender to my ways. For if you choose self-sacrifice,
giving up your lives for my glory, you will discover true life.
But if you choose to keep your lives for yourselves,
you will lose what you try to keep.'"*
Luke 9:23-24 TPT

<h1 style="text-align:center">32</h1>

Family Reflections

I spent time recently with my grandchildren, and my two year old granddaughter sat with me numerous times and repeatedly asked the same thing: "Poppy, I see your pictures?" She loves to look through the photos on my phone.

It is interesting that the first thing any of us do when looking at a group photo is to find ourselves. I sincerely dislike seeing photos of myself, so I disqualify as great any that include me. (If we doubt our own selfish pride, all it takes is one photo experience to bring us to reality.) Quickly, my girl Reese began to ask to see photos of family members (categorized and organized by faces thanks to Apple). As she looked through the photos, I transitioned from looking for myself in them to looking for the reflection of family lines in the faces.

My son has always favored my husband. When he was a child, I recall people recognizing him on the school playground as being the son of his father. Now he has a son that looks just like him. When I look through photos, I find myself remembering the smiles and expressions of the predecessor and reveling in the family lineage that is so readily apparent.

As I saw the photos of myself, I began to ask, "Will I lament over my face in the photo, or can I easily identify my Father as I reflect His face in my own?" I have wasted too much time and energy in my life avoiding my own reflection, but not focused enough on being the honest reflection of My heavenly Father in the earth.

Do I look enough like my Father while at the grocery store? Can people see the Father in my actions while at work? Do I re-present the Father to a world that is desperate for the healing and Life that He offers?

Too often, we spin our wheels trying to make ourselves look better, when our effort and our fascination should be solely on the One who gives us life. Matthew 6:33 TPT says, *"So above all, constantly seek God's kingdom and his righteousness, then all these less important things will be given to you abundantly."* "These less important things" are what we need in the here and now. God is telling us is to be captivated with His kingdom; be enthralled with His righteousness. When we are immersed in His light and His goodness, we will start to be a reflection of Him. We will look like Him, and the world will identify our family line!

"We can all draw close to him with the veil removed from our faces.
And with no veil we all become like mirrors who
brightly reflect the glory of the Lord Jesus.
We are being transfigured into his very image as we move
from one brighter level of glory to another.
And this glorious transfiguration comes from the Lord,
who is the Spirit."
2 Corinthians 3:18 TPT

33

You've been encumbered, dragging things behind you. You've moved forward, almost as if you didn't know you were dragging this giant sandbag behind you.

It was attached to you as a rope around your ankle, like shackles, scraping your flesh and creating scar tissue and hardened skin.

You've been such a trooper, working hard to go forward, and you've grown strong pulling the extra weight. You push ahead and have learned to jog and then to run, ignoring the baggage and the cumbersome package that you don't even notice anymore.

But I am setting you free from the weight that you've been carrying – dragging behind you. It doesn't matter anymore what you think is in the bag, what you put in there, what others stuffed in there when you weren't looking. Don't bother taking inventory of the things I'm taking. Just walk freely – stepping so lightly and skipping into your future with Me.

You'll move with Me effortlessly. Gone are the days when you'll have to strain and strive to move forward. You'll find yourself running ahead as I cheer you on and point and laugh at your incredible joy, and I'll share that joy with you!

You won't even remember the weight that constrained you in the past. You'll just revel in the path of freedom — unhindered, as you move and breathe and live life in Me.

"So if the Son makes you free, you will be free indeed."
John 8:36

"At last we have freedom, for Christ has set us free!
We must always cherish this truth
and firmly refuse to go back into the bondage of our past."
Galatians 5:1 TPT

34

Shine the Light

The cares of this world I have received as anxiety. Oppression sits on my shoulders like a heavy weight. In this season of fatigue, it would be easy to pull the covers over my head and take shelter in darkness. In this tent of isolation, I can momentarily block out the noise, but hiding does not change my life nor bring real peace.

You, oh Lord, are true and righteous. I make the choice to worship You. For You are creator of all. In my limited mind, I cannot comprehend the vastness of Your beauty, Your limitless creativity, nor Your powerful imagination. You speak, and the word goes on and on, accomplishing for eternity what You intended.

You said, *"Let there be light."* And there was light (Genesis 1:3), and there is light, and that light is continuing to go out and out and out, with no end. It drives forward, casting out darkness. And that also is the light of men: Jesus, the light of the world.

As we invite His light into every area of our lives, He drives out darkness. There is no battle for light to overcome darkness. The only struggle is for me to let the light shine through me.

"Then God said, 'Let there be light';
and there was light."
Genesis 1:3

"Then your light will break out like the dawn,
and your recovery will speedily spring forth;
and your righteousness will go before you;
the glory of the Lord will be your rear guard."
Isaiah 58:8

35

Hanging Banana Plant

I have a plant that hangs outside my front door. I bought it in the spring about 18 months ago. It is an interesting hanging succulent that I had never seen before, and I was very intrigued by it. I keep it by the front door because there I can see it the most often and visitors can view it as well.

One should understand from the outset that I do not have a green thumb. I love plants, but I am sadly not a great caretaker.

When I purchased this plant from a large nursery, it was thick and bright green and full of new growth. Over the previous winter, I moved it to the garage, and it faired okay. It didn't die, but it became thin and dull. This past spring, I moved it back to the front porch, but it never really regained its luster for life.

Now that I am about to move it to the garage in order to endure the coming winter, I thought I should do a little research. It turns out that this plant needs full light. Oh snap! That would explain why it struggled for the past nine months. Under my north porch, there is no direct sunlight. It has had enough light to survive, but not enough light to thrive.

There are times that this describes my spiritual life. I have enough light to support life because I have trusted Jesus and have Holy Spirit living in me. But if I'm not getting direct "Sonlight" daily, then spiritually I will become sparse and dull.

There are occasionally areas of new growth on my plant and seeing them gives me hope that it is still healthy. Sometimes in my spiritual life I will experience growth in a particular area, perhaps through new revelation or a message heard. But instead of leaning in to that growth and letting it wholly impact me, I will feed on it for a few days and then forget about it. If I truly want a greater impact, I may have to do something different.

I may need to look at the soil of my life, the foundation, the very building block of everything that it must support. I may need to add plant food or fertilizer, in the form of the written Word, prayer, study, or writings/messages from others. Ultimately, in this case, I need to move my plant. In order for it to flourish, it must have direct Light. I must move out of a place of complacency and convenience and into a place of actively seeking and receiving the Light.

It is convenient to have my plant on my front porch. It is easy to water it there and requires less effort and attention than if it were on the back porch. It is easily seen there by me and others. Even though it is visually available, it is not as visually appealing as it would be in another place where the observer would have to go to the effort to seek it out.

It is the same with us. We put things out for the world to see that may be satisfactory, but it is the deeper part of us that should multiply and bloom with life. If all that exists within us is what is readily seen by the casual spectator, we will live shallow and ineffective lives.

God has called us to increase, to blossom, to multiply! We need Light! We need to go beyond the convenient and dig in to what God has for us and His plan for us to push His kingdom forward. How am I created to influence the world for His glory? I must put in the effort to grow and become full and lush with His very Spirit in me. I must put myself in a position to be exposed to His Light.

Let's let Him shine on us and let's grow with an expectation of leading full and rich lives impacting others for Him.

In Him was life, and the life was the Light of men. The Light shines
in the darkness, and the darkness did not comprehend it.
John 1:4-5 NASB

once you were full of darkness, but now you have light from
the Lord. So live as people of light! For this light within you
produces only what is good and right and true.
Ephesians 5:8-9

36

Renew Your Mind

At the very time that your focus needs to be solely and wholly on me, your mind is like a pinball machine. Your thoughts are bouncing from one stimulus to another. And though you try to exercise your controls, they propel your thoughts back up and into the fray.

Step away from the game. At one time you were enticed by this mind play, exhilarated by the quick and exciting thought processes. But there is no rest for you here. There is no real fruit in your soul's amusement. It has become a drain on you, sucking your peace and leaving you weary and restless.

"Set your mind on the things above, not on the things that are on earth."
Colossians 3:2

Another way to say this could be "Intensively interest yourself in the things above-not in things on earth."

Look for Me; take notice of Me; hear Me. Renew your mind with the washing of My word, taking thoughts captive, grabbing them, and then judging whether they are in line with Me and My nature and word. If they're not in alignment, throw them out. Cast down vain imaginations and fruitless speculations. Don't spend your mental energy following trails of *what if.*

"... I came that they may have life, and have it abundantly."
John 10:10b

"… In this world you have tribulation, but take
courage; I have overcome the world."
John 16:33b

"Peace I leave with you; My peace I give to you;
not as the world gives do I give to you.
Do not let your heart be troubled, nor let it be fearful."
John 14:27

Take an interest in Me. Shift your focus and together we'll cause your thoughts to line up with Mine. Watch Me do a new thing in you. And watch Me produce real fruit in your life: joy, peace, patience, kindness, and self-control.

37

Jump!

I saw a carousel with music playing, going around in circles, surrounded by a wall where images were being projected. There were videos playing and a multitude of pictures flashing on all sides, telling a myriad of stories. I was standing between the two: the carousel and the wall of images.

The carousel represents lives that are going in circles with no real aim. There are different ways to ride and various looking modes, but ultimately, they are all going the same place, headed in the same direction, listening to the same circus music.

The images on the wall are messages of distraction from the enemy. With quickly-moving flashy pictures, Satan grabs our attention, telling us stories of potential, stories of other peoples' "better" lives, stories of our own failures. All of these are to distract us from the truth that everyone on the carousel is going nowhere. We are so drawn to the flashy photos that we have become complacent with the feelings of discontent that they produce in us.

The carousel is painted with pretty colors and sparkly jewels and tinsel. It is enticing to the passerby to get on and enjoy the ride. Eventually, some riders will recognize their plight on the ride: a life going nowhere, accomplishing nothing of real value, having no monumental role in the world, and forfeiting the life of adventure and distinction they imagined.

But it's easier to get on the carousel than to jump off, and being intimidated about the exit only leads to the rider's ultimate conformity in riding it out. He acquiesces, accepts his so-called plight in life, and submits to the ride. As I stood between the ride and the wall, I realized it was my choice. I could get on and enjoy the fake journey; I could be drawn in by the images on the screen and be lulled into a mindless stupor, entranced by nothing real or tangible.

I choose to live with vision, on purpose and for a purpose. I choose to look forward to destinations that cannot be seen from atop the carousel. And when I find myself going in circles and distracted by an enemy, I will lean into Holy Spirit and jump!

Revelation 21:3-5 NLT

38

Singular Focus

S et your gaze. Fix your eyes. There is only one plane/center point for the focus of a camera. Find Me in the center and let Me bring everything else into focus through the lens of My presence.

I am your lens and the refining filter of circulation. Everything else in your life flows through Me. I will weed out the things that don't belong if you will just allow Me. But that requires you to let Me work. Follow Me as I remove the muck and impurities, the things that have no place in you.

You are working with much dross, clouding the surface, and clogging the flow of your divine function. This sludge is heavy and tiresome. Let Me clear the way. I'm identifying elements that need to go, but you're not following through to release them and wipe them away.

Clear the surface: Release the junk; let it float to the surface as I draw it up. Then follow through and clear the surface. Like a skimmer net on the top of a swimming pool, together we will filter through the waters of your life. You'll be left with a purity of purpose, and you'll find an ease in serving and moving forward in My will.

"Therefore if you have been raised with Christ [to
a new life, sharing in His resurrection
from the dead], *keep seeking the things that are above, where Christ is,*

seated at the right hand of God. Set your mind and keep focused
habitually on the things above [the heavenly things], *not on things*
that are on the earth [which have only temporal value]."
Colossians 3:1-2 AMP

"And so, dear brothers and sisters, you are now
made holy, and each of you is invited
to the feast of your heavenly calling. So fasten your thoughts fully onto Jesus,
whom we embrace as our Apostle and King-Priest."
Hebrews 3:1 TPT

"My son, pay attention to my wisdom; listen carefully to my wise counsel.
Then you will show discernment, and your lips
will express what you've learned."
Proverbs 5:1-2 NLT

Simple Pleasures

See your spring irises. They stand against the elements and bloom with no effort from you. I did this. I know they bring you joy, and I delight in designing and creating situations and effects that please you.

It took no striving on your part to enjoy this simple pleasure. But to truly experience all there is for you, you'll need to stop what you're doing and take notice. Oh, you could merely drive by and glimpse their beauty, momentarily appreciating their unique color. And that would be enjoyable to you.

But to drink in all that is available in this scene, you'll need to stop. I can pour out as much as you want to drink in. If you want a quick sip, then give a passing look at what I have set up for you. But if you desire a refreshing and fulfilling taste of Me, then pause, and I'll fill you up.

I'll show you details and intricacies you've never noticed. I'll multiply your joy and reveal more of Myself to you. I long to be gracious to you. I literally rise, I get up from my seat, to show compassion to you.

So come to Me; lean in and drink of My goodness and My provision for you. Find contentment in Me. Be satisfied in the work of My hands for your good pleasure.

*"So the Lord must wait for you to come to him so he
can show you his love and compassion.
For the Lord is a faithful God. Blessed are those who wait for his help."*
Isaiah 30:18 NLT

"So faith comes from hearing, that is, hearing the Good News about Christ."
Romans 10:17 NLT

40

Great and Mighty Things

I am revealing Myself to you. You are dreaming dreams, hearing My voice, and seeing the plans I have for you. Though this revelation comes in bits and pieces, don't doubt its validity or its source.

"All your people will be righteous. They will possess their land forever, for I will plant them there with my own hands in order to bring myself glory."
Isaiah 60:21 NLT

"… At the right time, I, the Lord, will make it happen."
Isaiah 60:22b NLT

As you set your heart on Me, I'll continue to show you My own heart for you.

I will reveal great and mighty things - not to frighten you, but to encourage you, embolden you, and build you up.

You stand in what was once a museum of My presence, watching for the divine flow of My life washing over the now living stones of My people. A trickle has begun, and the river of life that flows down from the throne of God and from the Lamb is increasing in you, My people. In no time the flow of My presence will be evident, and I will draw people to Myself, like butterflies drawn to sweet nectar in a field of blooms. And I, Myself, will nourish them, grow them, and bring new fruit through them.

I will break through the mountain and carve a path like a giant waterfall. And My very hand will be upon it, creating light and illuminating My presence. I call out to you all: Jump into My presence. Immerse yourself in My glory and My unending love for you.

"Then he showed me a river of the water of life, clear as crystal,
coming from the throne of God and of the Lamb, in the middle of its street.
On either side of the river was the tree of life,
bearing twelve kinds of fruit, yielding its fruit every month;
and the leaves of the tree were for the healing of the nations."
Revelation 22:1-2

41

Real, Lasting Change

It is my belief that the grace of God working in me through the Holy Spirit gives me the power to change. It is transformation from the inside working its way out. If it's just me trying harder, then the change is short-lived and merely behavior modification. When change is Spirit-led, there is change that originates from beliefs (renewing my mind) and morphs into actions. Behavior, whether good or bad, is a result of what we believe. For example, I can say I trust God fully, but if my go-to is constant fear and worry, I need to question myself as to how fully I trust Him.

When I think about the process of change, I often think about the butterfly. As a caterpillar, he instinctively knows when to start preparing for his future home, the cocoon. Once he finds himself inside his personal encasement, he releases a mysterious enzyme that literally causes his own demise. The caterpillar dissolves. From this dissolution comes real transformation. The cells transform into that of a butterfly, and the insect re-grows into a beautiful new creation. The only problem is that the organism is stuck inside the closed cocoon. Now comes the battle. The butterfly must literally fight its way out of the chrysalis. And it is only through this process that fluid is transferred from the body of the butterfly and into its wings, causing them to strengthen and prepare for eventual flight. If this process is cut short or eliminated, the butterfly will lack the power to fly.

Once inside the cocoon, the caterpillar doesn't spend his existence stressing and groaning, wondering how he will ever change. The power to change comes from within. From inside him comes the release of the agent of change. From there, the miraculous happens. Transformation. Something new comes from that which submitted to the consecrated method.

Real, lasting change comes the same way in believers. The same Christ that saves us changes us. We have Holy Spirit within us who releases in us the grace that initiates and empowers transformation.

Lord, work inside me to bring the change that we both desire!

"And do not be conformed to this world [any longer with its superficial values and customs], *but be transformed and progressively changed* [as you mature spiritually] *by the renewing of your mind* [focusing on godly values and ethical attitudes], *so that you may prove* [for yourselves] *what the will of God is, that which is good and acceptable and perfect* [in His plan and purpose for you].*"*
Romans 12:2 AMP

"So all of us who have had that veil removed can see and reflect the glory of the Lord. And the Lord—who is the Spirit—makes us more and more like him as we are changed into his glorious image."
2 Corinthians 3:18 NLT

42

Metamorphosis Complete

Even as Holy Spirit has initiated and empowered change in us, we have to walk it out. He may have miraculously removed the desire for an old addiction, but we have the choice of whether to revisit it out of habit or boredom, or to stand in freedom from it.

When we're standing on the other side of change, we still have to make choices. Will we move forward in our new way of life, or will we open the door to old patterns and be drawn back into their clutches? Even in its escape from the cocoon, there is debris and remnants of the transformation. It's when the butterfly extends its wings and takes flight that it shakes off the remains of its process and sheds the useless and undesired garbage.

In our own transformation, there are remnants from the change that are still stuck to us. When we carry this waste and allow the fragments to cling to us, they can become unfriendly mementos and unwanted reminders, unlawful squatters that become more difficult to dispel. It's like being resurrected but walking in the new life wearing the grave clothes from which we've been set free.

Let's wash ourselves off, rid ourselves of the garbage from the past, and walk in the freedom for which we've been changed.

"It was for freedom that Christ set us free; therefore, keep standing firm, and do not be subject again to the yoke of slavery."
Galatians 5:1

*"For I am about to do something new. See, I have already begun!
Do you not see it? I will make a pathway through the wilderness.
I will create rivers in the dry wasteland."*
Isaiah 43:19 NLT

*"Don't copy the behavior and customs of this world,
but let God transform you into a new person by changing the way you think.
Then you will learn to know God's will for you,
which is good and pleasing and perfect."*
Romans 12:2 NLT

43

The Gift

My greatest gift to you is My presence. When I come, I bring it all: provision, grace, truth, gifts. What enables you to live victoriously is My ever-giving presence. I enable you to stand, to battle, to believe, to be all I've created you to be.

Just like a young child connected to her momma, she feels and senses and trusts that her mom is right behind her. Knowing that her mom is there frees her to be loving and joyful and engaging and brave and willing to share herself with others.

I am with you, just behind and beside and above. I am the foundation on which you stand. I am the vapor and the mist rising beside you. I am in the heavenlies giving you the covering that you so desperately need. I am the voice behind you saying, "This is My way; walk in it."

My sanctuary is forever in your midst.

"My dwelling place also will be with them;
and I will be their God and they will be My people."
Ezekiel 37:27

"Could there be any other god like Yahweh?
For there is not a more secure foundation than you."
Psalms 18:31 TPT

44

Moving My Focus

I come with such expectation, knowing that You're so faithful, so loving, desiring for me to hear Your voice. I'm almost overwhelmed with messages of love and affirmation from You! I almost can't separate one thought from another, bombarded with reasons to trust Your love for me, surrounded with this love. The words sound so shallow and simple, unable to describe fully the unified expression of Your thoughts toward me.

I feel as if I'm under a great waterfall with a million drops of Your love joining together in a cascade of life and joy and healing and empowerment, washing over me, touching every area of my heart and life. And even as I continue to be constantly nourished and filled by the living water washing over me, I find myself standing in a pool of this iridescent, life-giving water. Your anointing has covered me on every side, and now I stand on its foundation, looking only to You to fulfill every promise You've made.

There was a time when I would have been afraid of the onslaught of Your love and word to me, a fear of being overcome and lost under the waves of Your presence and power. Recognizing Your voice now and trusting Your love for me, I know it's not Your desire to push me down and hold me under, to suffocate or overpower me. Your love lifts me up and transports me from glory to glory, from one revelation to another. Like a rock skipping across the water, smoothly touching the surface – not fearing what's underneath – but moving forward to the next encounter, fully expecting that more is coming.

*"This is why I tell you to never be worried about your
life, for all that you need will be provided, such as food,
water, clothing—everything your body needs.
Isn't there more to your life than a meal? Isn't your body more than clothing?*

*"Consider the birds—do you think they worry about their existence?
They don't plant or reap or store up food, yet your
heavenly Father provides them each
with food. Aren't you much more valuable to your Father than they?
So, which one of you by worrying could add anything to your life?*

*"And why would you worry about your clothing? Look at
all the beautiful flowers of the field. They don't work or
toil, and yet not even Solomon in all his splendor
was robed in beauty like one of these! So if God
has clothed the meadow with hay,
which is here for such a short time and then dried up and burned,
won't he provide for you the clothes you need—you of little faith?*

*"So then, forsake your worries! Why would you say, 'What will we eat?' or
'What will we drink?' or 'What will we wear?' For that is
what the unbelievers chase after. Doesn't your heavenly
Father already know the things your bodies require?*

*"So above all, constantly seek God's kingdom and his righteousness,
then all these less important things will be given to you abundantly.
Refuse to worry about tomorrow, but deal with
each challenge that comes your way,
one day at a time. Tomorrow will take care of itself."*
Matthew 6:25-34 TPT

45

A Firm Foundation

In a vision, I see that someone rebuilt a deck on the back of a house. The deck was large and built with new wood. But in building it, they had evidently run short of materials. There was a square area where the boards were too far apart and were placed haphazardly and out of pattern with the others in an effort to make do with the supply on hand. In addition to being too far apart, the boards were insecure and wiggled when walked on. Although it was a relatively small area, it seemed like everyone needed or wanted to walk across the unsecure area. It left people feeling unstable and fearful. The foundation wasn't solid, and it immediately became apparent to those who stepped onto it.

I heard the Lord's admonition:

Check your foundation. Are you trying to make do with the supply you have on hand? Are you stretching your provision too thin? Are you skimping on the things that matter just to get done with the project at hand? Are you relying on your best guess or trusting in Me to lay a strong groundwork, the best foundation on which to build, and one that will sustain you and the people that share it with you.

Jesus is our sure foundation, an anchor in times of trouble and rough seas. The rock of our salvation.

"See me create a path for a trickle of water through the side of a mountain. Can I not make a way for you? Even now I am making streams in the desert, watering the dry places of hearts that long for a drop, in dry and thirsty places."

"Now, Lord, do it again! Restore us to our former glory!
May streams of your refreshing flow over us
until our dry hearts are drenched again."
Psalms 126:4 TPT

"Behold, I will do something new,
Now it will spring forth;
Will you not be aware of it?
I will even make a roadway in the wilderness,
Rivers in the desert."
Isaiah 43:19

46

You think an altar is an area at the front of a church where you go to feel sorry or want a reset with Me.

An altar is the place of My presence. The mercy seat sat in the middle of the Ark of the Covenant, between the cherubim. As they faced one another, My heavy presence settled there in a manifest way.

The weightiness of My presence.

The Hebrew word for *glory* means *that which is heavy or weighty.* Another way to say it would be My intense, profound presence; My sheer weight.

People think of Me as weightless. And because of My omnipresent nature, it would seem that way to your limited mind. But I am truth, I am the center of weightiness, drawing all things to Myself. As the earth's gravity pulls everything toward it, I am the very center of all things, majestically attracting all of creation back to Myself.

This is the altar: the pull inside yourself toward Me. Don't wait for a physical place or supposed opportunity, for now is the appointed time. Every moment with Me is a holy moment.

Recognize My presence and respond to the pull toward Me. Look in My direction and you'll be drawn by My love and compassion for you.

Meet Me at your altar.

"I am standing in absolute stillness, silent before the one I love,
waiting as long as it takes for him to rescue me.
Only God is my Savior, and he will not fail me.
For he alone is my safe place.
His wraparound presence always protects me
as my champion defender.
There's no risk of failure with God!
So why would I let worry paralyze me,
even when troubles multiply around me?
God's glory is all around me!
His wraparound presence is all I need,
for the Lord is my Savior, my hero, and my life-giving strength.
Trust only in God every moment!
Tell him all your troubles and pour out your heart-longings to him.
Believe me when I tell you—he will help you!
Pause in his presence."
Psalms 62:5-8 TPT

47

Low-Hanging Fruit

God, what do you want to say to Your child? Before I finished the question, I saw a banana tree. It was loaded with fruit at the top, and some fruit was falling to the ground to be enjoyed. I felt like God was saying,

> "You walk in such favor that you stand under the tree and good fruit literally falls into your hands. But the better fruit is up higher. Come up higher and I'll show you some good fruit! That doesn't mean striving to do something or working harder to get something. It just means *come up higher.*"

This is a Word for individuals, and it also a Word for the Church. I believe that He is calling us up higher. There is peace up higher; there is joy; there is comfort up higher. We will eat and survive if we stay on the ground, but to grow and thrive and enjoy the sweetest, most fulfilling fruit, we must go up, higher in the spirit realm.

I enjoyed a flight recently on a foggy, rainy day. I was disappointed that I would be unable to take advantage of the view from my seat by the window, as there was nothing to see because of the conditions. But as we climbed to greater altitudes, the light grew brighter and brighter, until we broke through the clouds, revealing a light so intense I had to draw my shade. This was a light so extreme its warmth permeated my shade and radiated into my being. There was sufficient light to function on the ground, but by rising higher in this circumstance, there was illumination beyond my capacity to take in.

There is such a stirring, such a weightiness, such a fullness in the Lord's invitation. It is an opportunity for people to get the breakthrough they have been waiting for. In these moments, we must suck all the life we can out of each opportunity. Take all there is and then ask for more, because there is always more.

"So I say to you, ask, and it will be given to you; seek, and you will find; knock, and it will be opened to you. For everyone who asks, receives; and he who seeks, finds; and to him who knocks, it will be opened."
Luke 11:9-10

"'For I know the plans that I have for you,' declares the Lord, 'plans for welfare and not for calamity to give you a future and a hope.'"
Jeremiah 29:11

48

Intimacy in Worship

You focus on melodies, notes, phrases, and rhythms. You look at your prescription for worship and think that if you fill all the compartments with the *right* elements, then I'll be pleased to accept your sacrifice of praise.

My only prerequisite for your sacrifice is your heart. I long for you to be free from the demand you put on yourself: the list of things that you think you must get in order so that your worship will pass the test.

Sit in My presence and position yourself to receive all I'm about to show you. Smell the aroma of My favor. Sense Me as I saddle up next to you and invade your space with My overwhelming peace.

Don't feel like you have to put your best foot forward. There's no pressure to perform with Me. Just bringing your humble heart to rest fully in Me is all I desire.

"O Lord, I will honor and praise your name,
for you are my God.
You do such wonderful things!
You planned them long ago,
and now you have accomplished them."
Isaiah 25:1 NLT

"Praise the Lord!
Praise God in his sanctuary;
praise him in his mighty heaven!
Praise him for his mighty works;
praise his unequaled greatness!
Praise him with a blast of the ram's horn;
praise him with the lyre and harp!
Praise him with the tambourine and dancing;
praise him with strings and flutes!
Praise him with a clash of cymbals;
praise him with loud clanging cymbals.
Let everything that breathes sing praises to the Lord!
Praise the Lord!"
Psalms 150:1-6 NLT

49

The Plunge Pool

Lord, Your love is like a waterfall of blessing! I can see it from a distance and be intrigued by its vast beauty and its massive power. I'm drawn to come closer as I hear the calming whisper from afar that there is peace in its waters.

The closer I come, the more I realize the magnificence of this glorious spectacle that is You. Even from a distance, I can feel the spray of the healing waters on my face. And though some would be put off by the sensation and others would be satisfied with this degree of intimacy, I am beckoned still closer.

As I come to the edge of the pool of Your love, I've now a decision to make. I'm near enough to view the cascading fall with clarity. I can see and appreciate its height and depth. I behold a rainbow of every color through the waters of the fall, and I'm reminded of all Your promises to me! The overspray now completely covers me, and the fresh clean smell of the pure waters and surrounding life fills my nostrils. I could stand here for an eternity and be content, enjoying the stunning view and every lush detail of this unique place, or I can follow my heart and Your invitation to come closer.

As I step into the clear cool waters, any trepidation about entering immediately leaves me, and the peace that's now covering my bare feet enters my being and migrates toward my heart. As I advance, You reveal the true identity of this basin: the plunge pool. Yes, Lord, I get it. I'm diving in.

Now under the flume of Your full, transparent, and unending love for me, my heart explodes with unspeakable joy. I am truly and completely surrounded by Your love.

Though in my flesh (body), I will walk about my daily life, in my spirit (the me that lives in You) and my soul (heart), I will remain here, transfixed on Your glory and experiencing life surrounded by Your mighty and vigorous love for me.

"But he who trusts in the Lord, *lovingkindness shall surround him."*
Psalms 32:10b

"But he who trusts in and relies on the Lord shall be surrounded with compassion and lovingkindness."
Psalms 32:10b AMP

50

Contentment and Peace

The peace extends from tree to branch
To leaves so lush and green.
To birds that call and bring to life
New grace their melodies sing.

The peace pervades the forest floor
And reaches the highest limbs.
The sun shines through with rays of light
Where dawn had been so dim.

The peace is almost tangible,
But just outside my grasp.
My mind goes back to similar times
To peace of ages past.

It seemed itself elusive,
This peace I'd sought before
By chasing means and things and dreams
It remained beyond the door.

From deep inside it called to me,
"Stop striving my peace to find.
It's in your Sabbath rest, you see,
You'll find real peace of mind."

So I turn to the life within
Where His Spirit waters and feeds.
And now I find that precious treasure
At last: contentment and peace.

51

Y ou are a worshiper.

This is not news to you. You've long known this about yourself, so this is not new revelation.

You've always assumed that you are a worshiper because you love music. You love to sing. You hear a melody in your head and are always filled with music. But every person who sings is not a worshiper. Every musician who plays his instrument skillfully is not a worshiper. Every person who listens intently to a beautiful sonata, enjoying the delicate movements and harmonies, is not a worshiper.

You are a worshiper because, at the instant you turn your attention to Me, whether in song or in prayer, it is then that your soul most lines up with your spirit. Your spirit is the part of you that is made new and righteous and holy in Me. You are in Me, and I am in you through your spirit. For now, your soul, which is your mind and will and emotions, is still a part of the kingdom of the earth. But when you enter into worship, it is at that time that your soul and spirit are most closely joined. Even your flesh is set aside in true worship.

And when you are in this place, worshipping in spirit and in truth, you see Me for who I am. You see that I am enough. You see that I love you and want only the best for you. You see that in Me you have everything you need or desire.

I love you so much that I gave you all of Me. I don't stop short. I created you in relationship with Me. You needed a Savior, and I gave My Son. You needed a comforter and helper, and I sent Holy Spirit.

> When you are afraid, I am your courage.
> When you are sick, I am your healing.
> When you are weak, I am your strength.
> When you are ashamed, I am your mercy.
> When you are discouraged, I am your hope.
> When you are lonely, I am your friend who sticks closer than a brother.
> When you are confused, I am your clarity.
> When you are lost, I am your light.
> When you feel defeated, I am your warrior.
> When you are in need, I am your supply.
> When you are in turmoil, I am your peace.

I gave you all of who I am. My love for you is so deep and so full and so encompassing that I gave you all of Me.

"O, taste and see that the Lord is good…"
Psalms 34:8a

"From now on, worshiping the Father will not be a matter of the right place but with a right heart. For God is a Spirit, and he longs to have sincere worshipers who adore him in the realm of the Spirit and in truth."
John 4:23-24 TPT

52

A Sweet Aroma

"I shall offer to you burnt offerings of fat beasts, with the smoke of rams;
I shall make an offering of bulls with male goats."
Psalms 66:15

Our worship has an aroma.

In Leviticus 1:7-9, God gave instructions to the priests about the protocol for sacrificing animals. Under the law, this was a mandated process that resulted in what God called a sweet aroma. Whether it was the burning of bulls or rams or goats or grain, it produced a sweet-smelling aroma to God.

How did the smell of the sacrifice differ from the scent of normal cooking of these same animals or flour? Occasionally, some special spices were used, but even when the meat was cooked without it, there was a difference.

It was a matter of the heart.

"… For God does not see as man sees, since man
looks at the outward appearance,
but the Lord looks at the heart."
1 Samuel 16:7b

God sees the position and the intent of our hearts. Though we only observe the spoken messages and the actions and behaviors of men, God has insight into the beliefs and desires and conditions of the heart.

This process of differentiated worship is true for us today. Hebrews 13:15 says that our praise to God is our sacrifice, because Jesus made the ultimate sacrifice as an offering for us, one time for all. We can now offer our worship in thanksgiving.

We don't cook meat as worship to God; we praise, and as we do, God sees our hearts. Just as the sweet aroma did not come from the beef or lamb or goats, it does not come from mere words or lyrics or melodies. What creates an aroma is the positioning of our hearts as we sing, as we share in generosity, and as we tell the story of Jesus with our lives.

God sees our intentions: to merely blend in, to mindlessly pretend, or to humble ourselves before Him in gratitude. God discerns our desires: to impress with grand words or to lead another into freedom in Christ. God understands our beliefs: that He is our everything, or that He is merely a means to a desired end goal.

So, whether you sing the age-old hymns or contemporary tunes, whether you sit quietly and bow or raise your hands high, whether you lay prostrate on the floor or jump up and down, or whether you pray to yourself or pray in public, let it be a sweet-smelling aroma to the Lord.

"...and walk in love, just as Christ also loved you and gave Himself up for us,
an offering and a sacrifice to God as a fragrant aroma."
Ephesians 5:2

53

Sacrifice of Praise

I know you are a right-on-time God. But our sense of timing doesn't seem to be gelling. I remember well the word about ingredients coming together in a full boil in order that they might meld together to bring a unique taste – much better than mixing the raw elements.

I feel like I am at full boil, to the point that I might begin to lose some substance if I overcook. I trust that You would never allow me to burn or come to ruin. I feel that, as I began this boiling process, some undesirable foam came to the surface and you were able to spoon it out, leaving the best and purest for your spectacular concoction.

I can only imagine the rich flavor that is to come as I pour myself out for You. Even now, I pray that the sweet aroma of my life rises to You in a sacrifice of praise.

So now I say, "Come, Jesus, and bring Your provision for my life. Bring the harvest of my seeds that were sewn in faith. Release the floodgates of heaven and let your bounty flow into me."

"Now to Him who is able to do far more abundantly beyond all that
we ask or think, according to the power that works within us."
Ephesians 3:20

"But seek first His kingdom and His righteousness,
and all these things will be added to you."
Matthew 6:33

54

You've found intimacy with Me addicting. You long now to steal away from life, to sit at My feet where you find refreshing. But I long for you to learn and experience My presence as you go about your work and as you handle your responsibilities. I long to intervene there, and you will hear My voice and feel My gentle hand as I guide your steps, even as you walk. You can move and be refreshed simultaneously.

I'm not a slot machine in which you put a coin and take a chance on winning. It's not a game – it's a relationship full of love and peace and communing with me.

You will see Me in unlikely places. You will hear My voice in unexpected circumstances. You will experience My presence at surprising times.

You have an expectation for the normal ways that I relate to you, and your faith pleases Me because I see your anticipation for our interaction. But I am expanding our interaction.

What excites Me about this season is that you are ready. When I give you the heads up that more of Me is coming, I know you'll be actively looking. You won't miss out on My presence or My direction or My crazy ways I share My love for you.

Father,
You are purifying hearts, You are purifying purpose,
You are doing a new thing requiring another level of

commitment and passion. I am putting it all out there for You to burn as a sacrifice. You will set fire to my sacrifice, and the things that are not useful will disintegrate; they will be consumed and will no longer be an obstacle/distraction for me. You will replace those things lost or given over with new anointing and exchange the ashes for gold.

Amen

"My child, will you treasure my wisdom?
Then, and only then, will you acquire it.
And only if you accept my advice
and hide it within will you succeed."
Proverbs 2:1 TPT

"As the deer pants for the water brooks,
So my soul pants for You, O God.
My soul thirsts for God, for the living God;
When shall I come and appear before God?"
Psalms 42:1-2

55

Fully Present in His Presence

It snowed last night. Just a dusting over the grass and trees. The wind is howling now, keeping me at the window to enjoy the beauty from inside my warm home.

I long to sit outside amongst the white magic that will so quickly be gone. I find it is that way with me: not satisfied to be inside – no matter what the weather - to merely view whatever is out there. I desire to fully experience things by immersing myself in the middle of the now.

Holy Spirit reminded me this morning that it is that way with Him. Many of us have been content to hear the forecast, to watch the beauty fall from inside our comfortable place, and to see the results from the window. But He is calling us to be fully present in His presence.

I want to plop my spirit right down beside Him. I will fully embrace all that He has for me. I will receive warmth for my bones, healing for my soul, and life in my spirit. In this space, I am surrounded by His unfailing love. And when I tune in, I can hear the angels proclaim, "… *Holy, holy, holy is the Lord God, the Almighty – the one who always was, who is, and who is still to come!*" (Revelation 4:8b NLT). He will speak words of life specific to me, and He takes delight in my being with Him.

The snow is fleeting, and the howling wind will eventually bring a warm southern breeze. The circumstances of our lives ebb and flow like the weather. But His nature, His presence, His call to us will never change.

Join me as we get outside of ourselves and live fully present in His presence.

Lord, in quietness and trust I will put my hope in You.

"You are worthy, O Lord our God,
to receive glory and honor and power.
For you created all things,
and they exist because you created what you pleased."
Revelation 4:11 NLT

"Because of God's tender mercy, the morning light from heaven
is about to break upon us."
Luke 1:78 NLT

56

overing. You didn't realize how much you valued covering until you had experienced it and then suddenly realized its absence.

Just as you grew up in the security and safety of home, you enjoyed the stability and the invisible shield around you that provided protection and peace of mind.

You equated that covering with the physical presence of someone big enough to fight for you. In depending on that physical presence, you didn't learn to feel for Me.

Now you feel uncovered. But this is a lie. I am your covering. Like a giant umbrella carried by an unseen attendant, I am constantly shadowing you, protecting you from elements that you'll never experience because of my faithfulness.

I have established Myself and My holy presence like a dome over your dwelling, a bubble of covering. Reside here with me and relish (cherish and savor) My peace.

"But in the depths of my heart I truly know that
you, Yahweh, have become my Shield;
You take me and surround me with yourself.
Your glory covers me continually.
You lift high my head."
Psalms 3:3 TPT

"His massive arms are wrapped around you, protecting you.
You can run under his covering of majesty and hide.
His arms of faithfulness are a shield keeping you from harm."
Psalms 91:4 TPT

57

Sweet Healing

I see a holy gauze. Knowing that many are in need of healing, I anticipate seeing many deep and painful wounds that are bleeding and oozing. But as I see the gauze lowered and then applied to the skin, I see no visible injury. And yet, God gently applies the bandage so carefully and lovingly to smooth, clear skin.

"My child, this is what healing looks like in the spirit. The need has already been met; the healing has already been provided and its work is done. In your flesh, you still perceive there's a booboo there; you still suspect a need yet to be met. And because I love you so much, I deal with you tenderly and mercifully. My touch is soft and brings comfort to you, and I place a bandage of protection over you as you realize the healing that has been accomplished in every weakness in your body.

"Let My sweet healing salve bring you peace as it penetrates and absorbs into your flesh. And when you readily remove the bandage, may you see for yourself the same healthy body that exists in truth: healing through and through."

Imagine if a whole community was open and looking, and God could reveal truth to them all. He might say, "You're good, but here's a bandage. Let Me love you."

"And He Himself bore our sins in His body on the cross,
so that we might die to sin and live to righteousness;
for by His wounds you were healed."
1 Peter 2:24

"'For I will restore you to health and I will heal
you of your wounds,' declares the Lord."
Jeremiah 30:17

"Oh, Lord God, answer my prayers! I need to see your tender kindness,
your grace, your compassion, and your constant love."
Psalms 69:16 TPT

"The Lord appeared to him from afar, saying,
'I have loved you with an everlasting love;
therefore I have drawn you with lovingkindness.'"
Jeremiah 31:3

58

Unseen Possibilities

"David came to Baal-perazim and defeated them there; and he said, "The Lord has broken through my enemies before me like the breakthrough of waters." Therefore, he named that place Baal-perazim."
2 Samuel 5:20

Baal-perazim means "Lord of the Breaks" or "Possessor of Breaches."

An Allegory of Breakthrough:

Frozen. Seemingly suspended in time. A frozen tundra of unseen possibilities. The magnitude of this expanse is grossly underestimated, as the proportion of what is visible is minute compared to the content that is outside human purview.

A mountain of rock has extended its broad fortification to hold back waters of advancement and gain. On one side, a body of lifegiving fluid. The waters churn with desire and anticipation of their progression onto a dry and thirsty land.

On the other side, a waiting. Praying, believing, declaring, preparing. An environment that has grown desperate for healing waters. Intermittent rains come and provide just enough sustenance to maintain life, but without the promised bounty and fullness that could, and should, be realized in abundance.

And just when the dwellers of this dry place could smell the waters on the other side of the obstruction, could feel the mist of its overspray, and join in the rhythm of its currents, the temperature began to drop. All hopes were dashed when the potential lifegiving source froze in place. The obvious reality of the new situation was impossible to ignore; without a massive change, the needed waters would never spill onto the perilous, wanting grounds.

The very condition that seemed to block and thwart their receiving of this valuable nourishment was altering the predicament by its very existence. An imperceptible phenomenon was taking place at the very intersection of the obscuring rock and the frozen treasure.

In warmer days prior to the frozen tundra, minute cracks in the mountain's structure had already received portions of the water, a confirmation of God's Spirit seeping into every nook and cranny. A holy soaking had taken place as the nectar pushed itself closer and closer toward those in anguish over the growing desolation. Now in the frozen expanse, underneath the surface, there was a splintering, a fracturing that was indistinguishable to the observer. But what was occurring in the bleakness of the deep would eventually be the catalyst bringing great reformation.

The cold despondency of the dark winter had brought with it sorrow and an impending doom. But God. In His goodness to work for their good, the dwellers of the dry heard the melody of promise "Change gonna come."

As the kairos season shifted, warmer winds prevailed, and a thawing began. The dwellers of the dry bargained, "If we can once again just enjoy the sound and scent of the waters, we will choose satisfaction. If only we could stand close and feel the mist of the moving currents, that could be enough!" Even as the melting took place there was an imperceptible transformation in progress: a softening, loosening, and relaxing in the mountain.

It was not until the ice was fully dissolved that the alteration could be seen. What began as small cracks in the rocks had grown to allow the passage of water between them. With an increasing excitement and rush of strength, the waters began to pound harder on the mountain of separation until a breach was realized.

Breakthrough! What began as a trickle of supply for the dry dwellers soon became a running estuary, an onslaught of blessing pouring through what was once their hindrance. The barrier had become a conduit of blessing.

"The breaker [the Messiah, who opens the way]
shall go up before them [liberating them].
They will break out, pass through the gate and go out;
So their King goes on before them,
The Lord at their head."
Micah 2:13 AMP

"And God is able to make all grace [every favor and
earthly blessing] *come in abundance to you,*
so that you may always [under all circumstances, regardless of the need]
have complete sufficiency in everything [being
completely self-sufficient in Him]
and have an abundance for every good work and act of charity."
2 Corinthians 9:8 AMP

"'For I know the plans and thoughts that I have for you,' says the Lord,
'plans for peace and well-being and not for disaster,
to give you a future and a hope.'"
Jeremiah 29:11 AMP

59

Transformed from *Glory to Glory*

ater, the moon shining on it, creating a thousand twinkling stars between its shores. A beautiful full moon. The clouds roll between me and the moon, sometimes shadowing its brilliant light, and then moving on, to leave only the clear light and the knowledge that nothing stands between us.

More clouds, some only thin, dimming its brilliance temporarily; some thicker, standing between us, hiding its power and light. The moon hasn't moved in that moment; although I've lost sight of its round figure, its light cannot be completely obscured. Its power still peeks out from every side of the rolling cloud.

My faith cries out, "It's still there! I know it is! I see evidence on every side!"

The cloud thins as it rolls on, and the light increases. I revel in anticipation, waiting as the light becomes brighter and the cloud becomes thinner, until I see the last of its shadowy tail. I am once again relishing the clarity, the beauty, and God's voice through His creation, the moon, as He calls out to me.

"I speak to you in every circumstance and every phase. I don't come and go. But you must listen differently as the clouds pass by. Sometimes you will hear and see Me with absolute and full knowledge, recognizing me for who I AM. Sometimes I will speak through the veiled curtains and shadows and a dimmed face. Sometimes you will look for Me and not readily notice My power and light. Others will think I am missing or uninterested. But you will know My place in the sky! You will sense My presence and hear My voice in a new way! You will be looking up, knowing that I am speaking, and you will hear. And as you hear My voice through layers of cloud, they will diminish. Your heart will be filled with joy overflowing, as you watch the layers of obstruction peel away. The expectation of what is to come—the great unveiling of My face—will bring unspeakable excitement. And through it—My face—you will be transformed into the same image, from glory to glory."

"But we all, with unveiled face, beholding as in a mirror the glory
of the Lord, are being transformed into the same image
from glory to glory, just as from the Lord, the Spirit."
2 Corinthians 3:18

"… Be strong and courageous!
For you will lead these people into the land
that the Lord swore to their ancestors he would give them.
You are the one who will divide it among them as their grants of land."
Deuteronomy 31:7b NLT

60

Keeping Focus

How cool would it be if I could be two places at the same time? I would like to be laying in a pool while simultaneously cleaning out my closet. I would like to be praying, journaling, and hearing from God while simultaneously accomplishing my laundry and housework.

God could have created us any way He desired. He could have given us unlimited abilities.

Even though He limited us physically to be in one place at a time, in our hearts and minds, we can be all over the map. And it does not take long to see the downfalls of this unique ability. This is a critical part of our choice, our free will that God granted us. We are not robotic; we get to choose our thoughts and the paths our minds follow. And to be effective, that requires focus, renewing our minds, and following Holy Spirit.

Scripture warns us of *"being a double-minded man, unstable in all his ways"* (James 1:8) [in everything he thinks, feels, or decides].

God warned the nation of Israel because *"their heart is divided* (Hosea 10:2 AMP)."

> *"Teach me Your way, O Lord;*
> *I will walk in Your truth;*
> *Unite my heart to fear Your name."*
> Psalms 86:11

So today as I do one thing at a time, I will focus on the challenge of keeping my mind going one direction at a time and keeping my heart fully undivided, open to His leading and direction.

61

You've grown comfortable in My presence, covering you like a warm flannel blanket on a cold morning. You readily recognize My voice, and you are diligent with the revelation I impart to you.

But you are inching into fear that I will cut off the sounds of My voice to you. You worry that this year of a new intimacy with Me will draw to a close, and I will stop speaking to you. Just beyond your conscience, you're secretly panicking that this was the best you're going to see.

Oh, My child, why in the world would I leave you in this place and stop communing with you? A good, good, Father wouldn't bring you to a new level of relationship and then walk away from his child.

This is only the beginning. Instead of slowing My communication with you, I'll expound. We're going deeper. You'll hear Me with more clarity. I won't stop speaking to you. I'll give you deeper revelation and insight and wisdom into My living, breathing word.

"Give ear and hear my voice,
Listen and hear my words."
Isaiah 28:23

"The sheep that are My own hear My voice and listen to Me;
I know them, and they follow Me."
John 10:27 AMP

62

Look Up, Child

Thorncrown Chapel is a glass house of God, built in the Ozark hills of Arkansas as a chapel for people to worship and experience the presence of God. It sits in the middle of the woods with glass walls and a glass roof, as if one were sitting among the elements to commune with God.

As I sat in a pew and took in the beautiful site and the exquisite architecture, I paused and waited for God to speak. I didn't want to visit such a lovely house of worship and not hear from God firsthand.

As I looked around the building's frame, I looked up at the glass ceiling, 48 feet into the air, seeing through it to a clear blue sky. Peeking over the top of the tall ceiling were trees swaying in the breeze, a surprising site to me. I expected to see only blue skies and a puff of white cloud roll by. But there, in some places obstructing my view of the sky, were trees, rising above and leaning over the top of this glass house. Immediately I thought of the verse,

> *"And he looked up and said, 'I see people,*
> *but* [they look] *like trees, walking around.'"*
> Mark 8:24 AMP

In the Bible, trees are sometimes symbolic of men. Psalm 1:3 NLT says, *"They are like trees planted along the riverbank, bearing fruit each season. Their leaves never wither, and they prosper in all they do."*

The next thought, I believe, was the word that I came to receive:

> "The ceiling of one man is the floor for another."

Glory to glory. One level of glory to another.

It is God's desire that we all be "*...conformed to the image of His son...*" (Romans 8:29b AMP). We are to be "*...transformed and progressively changed* [as you mature spiritually] *by the renewing of your mind...*" (Romans 12:2b AMP).

One level of glory to the next. Levels of spirituality make me a little uncomfortable. I'm not a competitive person by nature. I tend to shy away from situations that embody competition, or I sit in them but make light of my role so as not to appear either a winner or loser. But I've come to realize, in unpacking this word, that God's grand design is for us all to be just as His Son, a true reflection of Him.

Initially, I feel bad for the person whose ceiling is their measurement, their limit. And I am a little jealous of the one whose floor, whose standing position, is so much higher. One could easily make the mistake in assuming that these levels are about behavior and holiness and incidence of sin in the two different life examples. And it could be a reflection of that, not as a goal, but as a byproduct. It is so much more complex and layered than that.

The method by which we move from glory to glory is intimacy with Jesus. That intimacy produces fruit. That intimacy transforms us to be more like Jesus, changing our behavior, our goals, and producing holiness or living a set-apart life.

But there is more; there is always more! Other areas of our spiritual lives are also progressing from one level to the next. There are new levels of anointing, new revelations, greater awareness of Jesus at work in our lives, new ways of seeing and hearing from God, richer seasons of giftings from

Holy Spirit, deeper experiences in worship, and higher understanding of His word and its application in our lives.

If we stop short and assume that these levels are only about our behavior, then we're truly missing the opportunities in the other areas.

And the best part of all is that my winning, me moving up and forward, is never at another person's expense! There are no losers here by design. God has made it not only possible, but it His grand desire, that we all rise above our current ceilings and see them as floors for our next season. We can all remove the veil *"from our faces. And with no veil we all become like mirrors who brightly reflect the glory of the Lord Jesus."* 2 Corinthians 3:18a TPT

So look up, child, and see the trees looming above your present ceiling. Be enticed, be drawn, be motivated by His love, and then choose Him. Choose intimacy with Him and let Him lift you up to a new level of glory. Stand on what used to be your ceiling and reflect His face in new heights.

63

One Step Up

I see steps like layers of clouds making a way for my ascent.

The pull of this world is gravity's clutch. With great determination, I set my heart just one step up. As Jesus calls me forward, His grace empowers my feet to move, and I find myself on a new platform of vision and perspective.

I know this path is laid out specifically for me. Seeing its great expanse becomes daunting and doubt creeps in. Will I ever get higher? Can I manage the next step? The more I look at my own meager resources, the more I become fearful and want to pull back.

It is when I shift my focus back to the face and the call of Jesus that I sense His filling, and His voice beckons me forward, always forward.

"The steps of a [good and righteous] man are
directed and established by the Lord,
And He delights in his way [and blesses his path].
When he falls, he will not be hurled down,
Because the Lord is the One who holds his hand and sustains him."
Psalms 37:23-24 AMP

"It was like a dream come true
when you freed us from our bondage and brought us back to Zion!
We laughed and laughed and overflowed with gladness.
We were left shouting for joy and singing your praise.
All the nations saw it and joined in, saying,
'The Lord has done great miracles for them!'
Yes, he did mighty miracles and we are overjoyed!

Now, Lord, do it again! Restore us to our former glory!
May streams of your refreshing flow over us
until our dry hearts are drenched again.
Those who sow their tears as seeds
will reap a harvest with joyful shouts of glee.
They may weep as they go out carrying their seed to sow,
but they will return with joyful laughter and shouting with gladness
as they bring back armloads of blessing and a harvest overflowing!"
Psalms 126:1-6 TPT

64

When the veil was torn, I saw you, there in the outer court. You were so patient, waiting for your priest to do his work on your behalf. But as the veil *was rent in two*, torn from the top to the bottom, I saw your look of shock – to be standing face-to-face with Me. Soon that surprise turned to fear and then shame.

As I began to reach out to you, I saw you step back. Then as I called you by name, your eyes began to pool with tears. Our eyes met and you recognized My heart of love and peace that you'd only sensed before, but never actually gazed upon. With My arms open, I welcomed you as you ran to Me.

And now we can rejoice in this space of unrestrained love and unhindered freedom. Your only obstacle to the fullness of My presence is your availability and your willingness. I have opened the gate of My dwelling place to you and invited you to linger in this space of belonging. Let this sanctuary become your holy abode.

Look full into My face and find all the love I have for you. I am your supply, and every facet of Me is open to you.

> *"And* [at once] *the veil* [of the Holy of Holies] *of the*
> *temple was torn in two from top to bottom;*
> *the earth shook and the rocks were split apart."*
> Matthew 27:51 AMP

*"For now we see but a faint reflection of riddles and
mysteries as though reflected in a mirror,
but one day we will see face-to-face. My understanding is incomplete now,
but one day I will understand everything, just as
everything about me has been fully understood."*
1 Corinthians 13:12 TPT

*"Your pleasant path leads me to pleasant places.
I'm overwhelmed by the privileges that come with following you!
The way you counsel me makes me praise you more,
for your whispers in the night give me wisdom,
showing me what to do next.
Because I set you, Yahweh, always close to me,
my confidence will never be weakened,
for I experience your wraparound presence every moment.
My heart and soul explode with joy—full of glory!
Even my body will rest confident and secure."*
Psalms 16:6-9 TPT

65

Wasted Worship

I'm often like a petulant child who comes to Sunday dinner because it is there that I will get my week's allowance. Instead of engaging in the presence of the Giver and relishing the opportunity to pour out of myself in blessing to Him, I merely wait for His look my direction and then put my hands out, in the hopes that He will fill them. And He does.

Oh, how I've wasted precious moments at His table that I could've been lavishing my praise on Him, studying His loving expression, and soaking in the fragrance of His grace. I could have been searching the language for a fresh way to express His beauty and my love for Him. Instead, I too often lamented my own failures and shortcomings, focusing inwardly when the everlasting God was right before me.

Will He meet my need? Yes. Does He delight to give me the desires of my heart? Yes. But what joy He has when the desire of my heart is sincere communion with Him!

He longs for me to trust Him, but He also wants to entrust things to me. I must demonstrate a willingness to steward well His presence and His word, that He might entrust to me revelations and strategies and plans and assignments and hearts and souls of men.

But when these secondary things take precedence over the singularity and purity of loving Him, my worship is misplaced. How I long to be content at His feet without agenda. To linger in the sanctuary with the sound of many waters as He sings over His Bride. To cry anew with the angels, "Holy, holy, holy is the One who was and is and is to come! Worthy is the Lamb! You alone are worthy to receive all honor! Glory! Glory! Glory! You are majestic above all the earth!"

Let me never take for granted His willingness to be in relationship with me, the beauty of His overwhelming presence, and His awe-inspiring love for people!

Almighty God,

You are the Living Water! Plant me beside Your eternal stream, that I might be refreshed and sustained by You.

Grow my roots deep into Your Word that I would know that You are the Truth, the Light, and the Way. Keep me close that I would ever hear Your Voice like the sound of many waters. Comfort me in Your presence that might know the Peace of Your sabbath rest and live my days abiding in Your Love.

Amen

"…"Stand up and praise the Lord your God, for he
lives from everlasting to everlasting!"
Then they prayed: "May your glorious name be
praised! May it be exalted above all blessing
and praise! "You alone are the Lord. You made the
skies and the heavens and all the stars.
You made the earth and the seas and everything in them.
You preserve them all, and the angels of heaven worship you."
Nehemiah 9:5a-6 NLT

"Each of the four living creatures had six wings, full
of eyes all around and under their wings.
They worshiped without ceasing, day and night,
singing, "Holy, holy, holy is the Lord God,
the Almighty! The Was, the Is, and the Coming!" And
whenever the living creatures gave glory,
honor, and thanks to the One who is enthroned
and who lives forever and ever,

the twenty-four elders fell facedown before the one
seated on the throne and they worshiped
the one who lives forever and ever. And they surrendered
their crowns before the throne, singing:
"You are worthy, our Lord and God, to receive glory, honor, and power,
for you created all things, and for your pleasure they were created and exist.""
Revelation 4:8-11 TPT

66

Hidden Voids

T here's an area of your life that you've secluded. You've built a mound around it. This serves to hide it from peering eyes. It gives you satisfaction to let it remain hidden because then you aren't confronted with what you perceive to be a deficit. This mound that you believe is for your protection is actually serving to perpetuate the void. I long to plow down the raised ground, and to fill the voids in your life.

All of mankind was born "without," without My Spirit, My presence, and My life inside them because of the Great Fall. (Romans 5:12 NLT, "*When Adam sinned, sin entered the world. Adam's sin brought death, so death spread to everyone, for everyone sinned.*") But as soon as you put your faith in My Son, I filled that void. Since you now have My Holy Spirit within you, you are no longer "without."

Because you're human, you sometimes believe that there's still a lack that you need to fill by yourself. And just like Adam and Eve hid their nakedness in the Garden of Eden, you have an urgency to obscure or disguise your presumed inadequacy.

I am declaring to you, "You have nothing to hide!" Allow Me to dislodge the misused soil and use it to fill in the gaps. Here I will plant the seeds of restoration and wholeness and we will watch them grow together.

"Let every valley be lifted up, and every mountain and hill be made low; and let the rough ground become a plain, and the rugged terrain a broad valley; then the glory of the Lord will be revealed, and all flesh will see it together; for the mouth of the Lord has spoken."
Isaiah 40:4-5

"I have told you these things so that My joy and delight may be in you, and that your joy may be made full and complete and overflowing."
John 15:11 AMP

67

Give Thanks

Recently, I've considered the phrase *open-handed* as I've repeatedly heard these words in my mind and from others in passing. The idea of open hands is a reflection of generosity and a willingness to hold loosely the things of this life. If I'm not careful to guard my mind, I can slip into a scarcity mindset: "There's never enough," "There won't be enough," "What if I run out?" This way of thinking has me focused completely on the supply and not on the Supplier. My eyes are habitually looking for lack, shortage, deficit, and need.

When I walk in this attitude, even when my resources increase, I hold more tightly onto them. My fear mentality shifts from merely not having enough to losing what I have. And because of this concern, I close my hands into fists around the provision that I perceive will bring me peace and security. But even as I try my best, it seems that things keep slipping through my fingers like oil or grains of sand that my hands can't contain.

As a believer in Jesus, I look to scripture, and I listen for the voice of truth to lead me in how I should move through life on earth. It is interesting that the Bible teaches us that, as we listen and obey God's direction, many principles seem counterintuitive to what we would expect. The way up is down; the first is last; and leaders are the servants of all.

As I begin to understand this foundational belief system, Luke 6:38 TPT can become a way of life: *"Give generously and generous gifts will be given back to you, shaken down to make room for more. Abundant gifts will pour out upon you with such an overflowing measure that it will run over the top! The measurement of your generosity becomes the measurement of your return."*

Don't misunderstand; we don't give to get! We give out of the overflow of God's blessing to us, and we become the conduit through which He lavishes His love and grace and provision on a world in need. The more we give, the more He entrusts us to give.

There are some things to which we should hold tightly. The Bible says to hold fast to the hope we have in Jesus. Hold fast to that which is good; cling to the Lord; hold on to confidence in His promises. These are things that we, as followers of Jesus, will clutch to our hearts and not release. We must discern what to squeeze our fist around and the things for which we keep open hands.

I want to live open-handed. I want to be expectant and ready to receive the goodness of God and be ever thankful to Him. In gratitude, I want to be on the lookout for His divine supply to pour into my open hands. Then I want to keep them free and unrestricted so that I serve as a pipeline of His blessing flowing onto others. This will be my greatest thanksgiving.

"But many who push themselves to be first will find themselves last.
And those who are willing to be last will find themselves to be first."
Matthew 19:30 TPT

"So now wrap your heart tightly around the hope that lives within us,
knowing that God always keeps his promises!
Discover creative ways to encourage others
and to motivate them toward acts of compassion,
doing beautiful works as expressions of love."
Hebrews 10:23-24 TPT

68

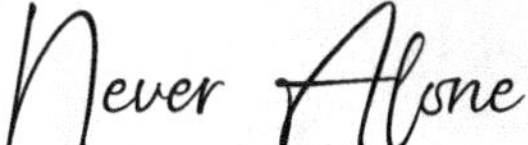

Never Alone

I can see that you are lonely and afraid. I know what it is to be lonely. Oh, I had friends around Me (disciples) and lots of crowds that followed, but no one could really comprehend My struggles and My trepidation about what I knew was to come. I remember longing for someone to share in My trials and pain. I also know how it felt when the one closest to Me couldn't stand under the pressure. Oh, I knew it was coming, and I'd even warned him, but it hurt, nonetheless, maybe even more than rejection of those who never really trusted in Me in the first place. But all is well. And still, I'm especially fond of My dearest friend, Peter.

You see, hurt comes in many ways, many completely unintentional. But a generous spirit and forgiveness comes in just as many ways; more, really. Whether it is the pain of feeling left out, the pain of being abandoned, or the pain of being betrayed, there's grace sufficient in Me.

I would never desire that you suffer in being alone, but I do see an opportunity for a beautiful season of intimacy with Me. I understand your longing for friendship and companionship with others; I have that same longing for you. I desire to walk with you as I did with Adam in the cool of the evening and show you beautiful truths.

Let's relax on the patio with a cup of coffee, for you of course. I'll begin to download a vision of My love for you. I'll speak to you of wonderful works that I've prepared ahead especially for you.

Cease your striving in busyness and worthless time wasters. You call them screens. Remember My words not to worry about what you'll wear or what you'll eat; today you call it shopping and take out. Not that those things are evil in and of themselves, but they aren't your focus. If they are, it's a shallow life you will live, and I have so much more for you.

Come to Me; meet with Me; sit with Me; hear Me; learn from Me; share with Me; take from Me; be with Me. Soon you'll see that we've become one. You will begin to say what you hear Me say and do what you see Me do. You'll move aside, and together we'll live this life as I love people through you and use you to advance My kingdom in this world.

"For we are His workmanship, created in Christ Jesus for good works,
which God prepared beforehand so that we would walk in them."
Ephesians 2:10

"O God of my life, I'm lovesick for you in this weary wilderness.
I thirst with the deepest longings to love you more,
with cravings in my heart that can't be described.
Such yearning grips my soul for you, my God!"
Psalms 63:1 TPT

69

Heart Choices

When we accept what Jesus has done for us and receive Him into our lives as Lord, the Bible describes what God supernaturally does in our lives.

"Moreover, I will give you a new heart and put a new spirit with you;
and I will remove the heart of stone from your
flesh and give you a heart of flesh.
I will put My Spirit within you and [I will] cause you to walk in My statutes,
and you will be careful to observe My ordinances and do them."
Ezekiel 36:26-27 AMP

God has replaced my heart of stone and given me a heart of flesh. There are days when it would be more comfortable to live with that old heart of stone. In the interest of self-protection and avoidance of pain, a stony heart is sometimes desirable. But here I stand with this heart of flesh, for which I choose to be grateful. Some days it feels as if my chest has opened wide to expose this flesh, and it is vulnerable to the penetration of darts from an unseen enemy. Even light scratches from an unintended perpetrator further damage this heart of flesh.

My choice is whether to allow my heart to become hard again, to leave my heart soft and pliable, or to hide.

Without proper attention to fresh wounds, they will become scabbed over, eventually turning into callous scars, creating areas of my heart that are rigid and impenetrable. Operating with a hard heart limits me in every area of life. It limits my ability to relate to others, to love them openly and fully, and to live out my purpose. It is only in cooperating with Holy Spirit and choosing to receive the healing He provides that I can remain healthy and keep my heart soft and pliable.

Another option, short of becoming hard again, is to hide. I can choose to overprotect my heart and cover it with a shell of self-preservation and self-defense. I can manipulate and hold others at bay, wrongly assuming that a lack of discomfort is abundant life. I can buy into the lie that not experiencing pain equals comfort by default.

But by hiding, I'm forfeiting my assignments that God has laid out for me. His word says,

"For we are His workmanship, created in Christ Jesus for good works, which God prepared beforehand that we would walk in them."
Ephesians 2:10

He has specifically designed things for me to do, people for me to impact for His glory. If I spend my life hiding and protecting myself, I may avoid hurt and disappointment, but that comes at a great price.

My other option is to join with Jesus, receive the heart of flesh, and then let His peace guard my heart and mind (Philippians 4:7). I can choose, even through pain, offense, and wounds from others, to let Holy Spirit bring His healing salve and renew my heart. I can lean in, press on, and let Him bring the healing and peace that I so desperately need. This is grace in action, doing for me what I cannot do for myself. And when I let Him, He is faithful to renew my heart of flesh, leaving it pliable, yet strong.

I choose healing and God's peace. Come, Holy Spirit, with Your healing salve and renew this flesh, leaving it pliable, yet strong.

70

Why are you afraid to ask Me some questions? There are some issues you bring to Me, desperate for answers. You sit so intently before Me, hanging onto My every word, listening for not only the instruction, but also the nuance in My voice.

But I sense there are other issues you avoid with Me. It's as if you're dreading My supposed answer, assuming or anticipating a negative response from Me. I'm not referring to questions of character or sin or beliefs, but just daily tasks, opportunities, or circumstances.

Sometimes I think you forget that I take joy in your joy. I have only the best plans for you, I want only what will bring you true life and multiply the grace and truth within you. I don't withhold good things from you, and I don't desire to keep you in a box tied up with ribbon and bows, appearing acceptable to the rest of the world.

So, ask away, knowing I'll lead you through the best life.

I won't be manipulated by your fear but will be moved only by your faith and by My unending love for you.

"And without faith living within us it would be impossible to please God.
For we come to God in faith knowing that he is real and that he
rewards the faith of those who passionately seek him."
Hebrews 11:6 TPT

71

Fear distorts your vision. In My word, I addressed fear one time for every day of the year. It's no small thing that I would speak to you about it so much.

When you haven't learned how to apply My truth about fear, which is My perfect love and your complete trust in it, you won't see clearly. Not only will things look vague and uncertain, but you will see the wrong things. You'll take note of situations, circumstances, pictures, and words and wrongly credit them as being from Me.

Take the blinders off. Clean the lens of your heart. I'm not trying to scare you. I'm not chasing you with gnashing teeth and a gun pointed at your head. I'm not into intimidation tactics. I am here to love you, to draw you to Myself for your good.

Come to Me and lean into the fullness of My presence, grace, joy, and love for you. Don't mix in your stuff -- anxiety, fear, doubt -- with My presence, peace, joy, and love.

Trust My ability and desire to bring resolution for your issues and My goodness into your life. I am surely enough for you -- only Me. You have all provision in Me, and I've already given you all you need. Stand under the cascading power of My love and watch me drive out fear and replace it with My truth.

*"For God did not give us a spirit of timidity or cowardice or
fear, but* [He has given us a spirit] *of power and of love and of
sound judgment and personal discipline* [abilities that result
in a calm, well-balanced mind and self-control]."
2 Timothy 1:7 AMP

*"We use God's mighty weapons, not worldly weapons,
to knock down the strongholds of human reasoning
and to destroy false arguments."*
2 Corinthians 10:4 NLT

*"'No weapon that is formed against you will succeed;
and every tongue that rises against you in judgment you will condemn.
This* [peace, righteousness, security, and triumph over opposition] *is
the heritage of the servants of the Lord,
and this is their vindication from Me,' says the Lord."*
Isaiah 54:17 AMP

72

Beware: The Predator

There is always a presence of multiple options. Thoughts are like birds: you can't control what flies over your head, but you can prevent one from making a nest in your hair. We have an abundance of opportunities to follow. We must quickly distinguish those that produce life and those that will lead to death.

There is the voice calling quietly to us from the heights of His perch. He makes no fuss to get our attention; He just persistently calls.

There are those voices flying and flapping their wings around us. And lest we should ignore them, they come at us, swooping, and causing no small stir. They take us from our tasks, grabbing our attention, until we find ourselves flailing our own arms in an effort to shoo them away. Our focus is now out the door, and with it has gone our peace. These voices are more than an annoyance; they are a weapon of distraction.

But as we give attention to these irritating rascals, we don't notice the newest addition to the mind-bending party: the predator. He is quiet, and he slips in when our attention is drawn away from the responsibility of guarding mind and heart. Our eye is so engrossed by the flurry and commotion of the distraction that we are now vulnerable to real danger. We have become fatigued, and as a result, we are exposed. Destruction is now crouching at the door. Disregarding his presence and failing to identify this real threat will open the door for him to come in for the kill.

What to do? Identify the real threat. *"For our struggle is not against flesh and blood, but against …spiritual forces of wickedness in the heavenly places"* (Ephesians 6:12). The enemy of our soul will use any means against us. Distinguish between the whirling, peace-stealing diversions, and the death-producing terrorist.

Draw your sword, both the written and the spoken word of God. It is the light of His presence that produces the power to push back the darkness. Renew your mind through the washing of the Word. Align and position yourself to hear the soft call of Him and He will annihilate the weapons of the evil one for you. Fight the good fight of faith. Discern the battles and stand. And when you have done all you can do, stand.

Then, the Father will speak words of restoration and refilling. These will hover in front of us like an invitation to see and follow into union with Him and the serenity He lavishes on us. His supply is ample and unending.

"Be well balanced and always alert, because your enemy, the devil,
roams around incessantly, like a roaring lion looking for its prey to devour."
1 Peter 5:8 TPT

"For we are not fighting against flesh-and-blood enemies,
but against evil rulers and authorities of the
unseen world, against mighty powers
in this dark world, and against evil spirits in the heavenly places.
Therefore, put on every piece of God's armor
so you will be able to resist the enemy in the time of evil.
Then after the battle you will still be standing firm."
Ephesians 6:12-13 NLT

"For the Lord God helps Me,
Therefore, I am not disgraced;
Therefore, I have set My face like flint,
And I know that I will not be ashamed."
Isaiah 50:7

73

Don't Forfeit Peace

You are fighting some battles that aren't yours. You are getting sucked into a mindset of confusion and overwhelming feelings, and then you're stepping into fear.

I see you walking along My path on stones laid just for you to tread. Somewhere, just beyond your vision or reach, is a snare. It's not on your path at first, but you become entranced by it. A passing glance to the side becomes a steady search for the source of the distraction. The harder you look, the more likely you are to find what you're seeking. A momentary powerless call from the enemy becomes a shouting match between you.

At times you leave my well-designed trail to chase an elusive and clever foe. At times, you entice him onto the path with you, only causing you to stumble as you focus on him instead of Me and where I am leading.

In both instances, you've forfeited peace. You've handed over your direction as you jab and punch at this enemy instead of moving forward.

There will be battles that are yours; that is why you've been given My armor. I will fight alongside you. In either case, I'm not leaving you. I've got your back. I will show Myself strong on your behalf.

But why waste your God-centered serenity by engaging in unnecessary scuffles? Stop battling the enemy over a perceived injustice that hasn't happened. Stop anticipating and preparing for arguments that shouldn't take place. Stop giving precious mental space to fruitless rationalizations.

Look at Me. See Me. Hear Me. I will show you how to maneuver through situations on your path. I'll give you divine strategies that you could never conjure up on your own. I will show you the way to light and life: real lasting abundant life in Me.

"We are destroying sophisticated arguments
and every exalted and proud thing
that sets itself up against the [true] *knowledge of God,*
and we are taking every thought and purpose
captive to the obedience of Christ"
2 Corinthians 10:5 AMP

"But have nothing to do with foolish and ignorant speculation
[useless disputes over unedifying, stupid controversies],
since you know that they produce strife and give birth to quarrels."
2 Timothy 2:23 AMP

74

Whack-A-Mole

Have you ever played the game where you look at something for several seconds, then close your eyes, and an image forms that you see with your eyes closed? The image does not look like the original; it is some sort of reflection of it, but changed.

Very early one morning, before I had an opportunity to open my eyes to the still darkness around me, I saw a floor. It was a hardwood floor, but a bright and unattractive pale yellow in color (one you'd never see in a house). There were dark brown, noticeable notches in the floor.

The word "distortion" came to my mind.

The Lord says, "You are standing on a foundation that is distorted. You are deceived at the root, and it has become the lens through which you see and operate."

How does one know when one is deceived? How does one identify distortion? I can recognize distortion when I compare it to the original, the true version. I can identify a lie (misconception, error, or twisted belief) when I hold it next to the truth. Where do I find the real truth? The Word of God.

Unless someone points me to the truth, I will continue to build upon the deceit and distortion in my mind or heart. When it becomes the foundation on which I build my life, then everything on top of it is subject to collapse.

We can easily see the effects that come from this pattern of building on distortion: chaos, destruction, unsteadiness, double mindedness, and further deceit. Consider a house that is built on sand, with a shifting foundation. It may appear solid, even enticing, after it is first constructed, but with time, cracks will appear in the walls and ceiling. Walls will begin to separate from each other, creating an opportunity for bugs and pests to come and go. As the house continues to move, even critical infrastructure will be affected as pipes can break and cause damage that affects the entire building.

A contractor can patch and repair these visible issues and even address pipes and stop the flow of unwanted water or sewer (whole different issue) through the house. But without addressing the root - the foundation – he cannot prevent further damage. It's like playing the game Whack-A-Mole. It pops up, we respond, and then it pops up somewhere else.

It's much more difficult to identify the source and repair the foundation. This takes wisdom, and diligence, and effort, and hard work. But unless we go to the foundation, we're destined to continue the Whack-A-Mole game, addressing outward symptoms as they appear.

Let's ask ourselves, am I seeing symptoms of an errant foundational belief? Here's an example. Lie: I am not worthy. Symptoms: I'm constantly trying to prove my value to other people. This can be done through striving and overcompensating. Less healthy symptoms can be putting others down to elevate myself, manipulation, or in seeking attention by repeatedly putting myself down in an effort to get someone else to build me up.

When we see the symptoms manifest in our lives, we must identify the root. Then we must compare that belief to the truth. It is only then that we can know if it lines up with God's word or is a lie, a distortion.

But we have to be diligent, to put in the effort and hard work. We always need insight from Holy Spirit, who reveals all truth (John 16:13). Sometimes we need the wisdom of others, from godly friends or trusted professionals – not from people who suffer from the same symptoms. (If I need financial advice, I should go to someone who is financially secure and demonstrates wisdom, not someone who is in the same sinking boat as me.)

Once we identify the distortion, we must remove the lie and replace it with the truth. Then we must begin building anew on the true, strong, established foundation. Anytime we see an old symptom, we quickly recognize it and deal with it by taking it back to our renewed root, and our brand new beautiful floor that is sturdy and strong!

"For no one can lay a foundation other than the one
which is [already] *laid, which is Jesus Christ."*
1 Corinthians 3:11 AMP

"You are rising like the perfectly fitted stones of the temple;
and your lives have been built up together upon the foundation
laid by the apostles and prophets, and best of all,
you are connected to the Head Cornerstone of the building,
the Anointed One, Jesus Christ himself!
This entire building is under construction and is continually growing
under his supervision until it rises up completed
as the holy temple of the Lord himself.
This means that God is transforming each one of you into the Holy of Holies,
his dwelling place, through the power of the Holy Spirit living in you!"
Ephesians 2:20-22 TPT

"When the Spirit of truth comes, he will guide you into all truth.
He will not speak on his own but will tell you what he has heard.
He will tell you about the future."
John 16:13 NLT

"Your Word is truth! So make them holy by the truth."
John 17:17 TPT

75

Sustaining Grace

I'm trying to protect your ears. There are some things that I am closing off from your hearing because they are untrue, unhealthy, and will only produce negative fruit in you.

But I can't protect you from you. Your own inner voice is speaking recrimination, ineptitude, and fear. I have provided you with choice and free will out of My goodness. I've put My Spirit in you, and the same grace that saved you sustains you. It enables you and empowers you to take every thought captive and put it through the filter of My word and My character. I have provided you with the tools to renew your mind and transform it for My glory.

Don't give place to the fear of coming doom. Don't waste your energy on mental calisthenics and exercises of futility, arranging arguments and rationalizations that produce only dead things: frustration, dread, and more fear.

I want to help you in this, but you control what you allow in and focus on. Help Me help you. Change your view and turn the dial on your inner radio. Set My voice above the others and look to Me. Tune in to Me.

"Trust in the Lord completely, and do not rely on your own opinions.
With all your heart rely on him to guide you, and he will lead
you in every decision you make. Become intimate with him in
whatever you do, and he will lead you wherever you go."
Proverbs 3:5-6 TPT

"So above all, guard the affections of your heart,
for they affect all that you are.
Pay attention to the welfare of your innermost being,
for from there flows the wellspring of life."
Proverbs 4:23 TPT

76

You formed me in the womb
Before I knew your name.
You set the days ahead of me
Before any of them came.

I heard you call me gently,
And I answered right away.
You joined your Spirit to me
And promised that You'd stay.

As a child, I saw your heart
that looked like purest love.
The more I understood
Confirmed it from above.

As I moved from milk to meat
My appetite did grow.
I longed for more than time with You;
I yearned Your face to know.

Ever in Your mercy
You met me at my need.
And gave me more of grace,
A fragrance that I breathe.

Now we walk as hand in hand A
Friend stands by my side.
You've become my full supply, As
I become Your bride.

We move from glory to glory
With each step I take toward You.
I'm drawn into Your presence
As You make all things new.

77

Tuned In

We are blessed to have a windmill close to our home, and it brings me so much pleasure to look out my front windows and watch the sun set beside it.

It's an old windmill. I can tell this by the way it looks, and I can tell this by the way it squeaks. It's not an offensive sound, but as the big blades turn with the wind, there's a definite high-pitched song that it sings.

What I can't do is see the windmill from my back patio. The patio is my favorite place, especially for morning coffee. While I can't see the windmill, I can easily hear its squeak.

One morning as I sat in my favorite chair with a journal and a cup of coffee, enjoying a fall breeze, there were many thoughts and concerns that filled my mind. I sat for several minutes addressing responsibilities, a friend's request for prayer, and mulling the cares and concerns that wrestled for my attention.

It was only after I (eventually) began to quiet my thinker that I heard the sweet sounds of the windmill. As I considered this new sound within my consciousness, I realized that the wind had been blowing all along, but I hadn't noticed the sound. Once I became aware of the windmill's song, I couldn't unhear it. Now the squeak continued, and I heard each turn of the blades.

My mind was tuned in to the sound. It was there as a backdrop even as I focused my attention in several other directions.

I think this is similar to the voice of Holy Spirit. I believe He is always speaking but we often don't hear because of the distractions in our own hearts and minds. When we quiet our souls, we can tune in to the sound of His voice. The more we listen, the more we will hear. Mark 4:25 says, *"For whoever has* [a teachable heart], *to him more* [understanding], *will be given; and whoever does not have* [a yearning for truth], *even what he has will be taken away from him."*

Just as I began to listen intently and hear, I can also ignore the sound, move my focus, and give my attention so fully to something else that it will drown out the windmill's squeak. We have the same choice with God's voice. We can listen solely for Him; we can proceed with our tasks and function in this world while still acknowledging His sound and listening for His direction; or we can tune out by listening to our own will or emotions.

Let us be intentional about dialing in and listening for His voice. And when we realize that we're not in tune and in step to hearing Him, let us quickly refocus our attention back to Him to hear the song He sings over us and the direction He gives.

"For the Lord your God is living among you. He is a mighty savior.
He will take delight in you with gladness. With
his love, he will calm all your fears.
He will rejoice over you with joyful songs."
Zephaniah 3:17 NLT

Transition

Change is hard. Even good change is hard. There is artificial comfort in standing still, and you can delude yourself into believing that you can't fall if you don't move.

There are some seasons when I encourage you to move, and I reveal where your next step is to be, but you dig your heels in and say to yourself, "I choose safety over obedience." Eventually, My beloved child, the ground will crumble beneath your feet, and you'll have a decision to make that will seem sudden and out of the desperation of necessity.

It is true that change is inevitable for every living being, but the plan I have for you is good; it is ultimately for abundant life. My design is from glory to glory.

I am calling you into a new realm of My presence, a new space in My throne room. I am introducing you to a new tone in My voice. You will hear a lilt in My proclamation that will bring you great joy.

So, do not waste time on empty contemplation but meditate on My word and My face. Hear My call and follow My voice.

"He opens before me the right path and leads me along in
His footsteps of righteousness so that I can bring honor to His name."
Psalms 23:3 b TPT

79

Don't Quit

I train lifeguards. Before a student can enter a lifeguard training course, he/she must pass a skills test. During the final portion of the three-part test, participants must tread water for a period of time without using their hands. I time the test on my phone, calling out, "one minute, two minutes.…"

All potential students are instructed to go to the middle of the diving well and, when given the signal, to lift their hands out of the water to prevent using them during the time period. During one training course, we began the test; one minute, two minutes went by. As we were nearing the end of the test, one student began to get closer and closer to the edge of the pool. One of the co-instructors called out to her, "Don't quit; you're almost there! Don't quit!" When she got too close to the edge, her foot grazed the bottom slant of the wall. She immediately reached out with her lifted hand and grabbed for what she instinctively felt was the safety of the wall.

Game over. Unsuccessful. A mere 17 seconds remained. When I told her this, her reaction was as you'd expect. "Oh man, I could've done it 17 more seconds! I was just so close to the wall, and when my foot felt the bottom, I grabbed the side and gave up."

Immediately I thought, "How many times have I given up spiritually and settled for the seeming security of a known boundary?" We believe and pray for breakthrough in an area, but we can't see a clock, a timeline, and we stop short. We give up when what we were declaring and believing for was just around an unseen corner.

If only the swimmer had remained in the center of the diving well as I'd instructed.

Sometimes the best place for us is to be in deep waters with God as He gives us our foundation, and His living word is our boundary and guide. If we are reaching down to touch the floor, how will we rise to fulfill His call to a new thing?

If we are to experience breakthrough in an area of our lives, we must remain in alignment with where He has instructed us to be. The swimmer succumbed to temptation to take hold of the pool's edge because she had left her initial position and was within arm's reach of the ledge.

God has given each of us directives, and then He calls out encouraging us. "You can do this! Stay with it! Don't quit!" But when we fail to remain in position, in alignment with Him, we move closer and closer to giving up. We reach for the known or familiar handhold just before our promotion or freedom or promise manifests.

If only we could see the clock, if only we could see with our spiritual eyes the few steps in front of us to the awaited prize. But that is faith. Hebrews 11:1 NLT says, *"Faith shows the reality of what we hope for, it is the evidence of things we cannot see." Faith* in Hebrew means *truth, stability, certainty.* We must get to the place where we trust God more than what we see in the natural.

May we all move out into deep waters to which He's called us. May we keep kicking: keep praying, keep believing, keep declaring. May we hear Him call out to us and receive His cheers, His support, and His urging toward our breakthrough. May we trust Him above everything that we can see or touch in the natural. And may we all revel in His exclamation of "Well done!"

"Trust in the Lord with all your heart and do not
lean on your own understanding.
In all your ways acknowledge Him, and He will make your paths straight."
Proverbs 3:5-6

"For the sinful nature has its desire which is opposed to the Spirit,
and the [desire of the] *Spirit opposes the sinful nature;*
for these [two, the sinful nature and the Spirit] *are in direct opposition*
to each other [continually in conflict], *so that you* [as believers]
do not [always] *do whatever* [good things] *you want to do."*
Galatians 5:17 AMP

"For God has not given us a spirit of timidity, but
of power and love and discipline."
2 Timothy 1:7

80

The Way to Peace

One word from Me can bring a lifetime of clarity. It is My sincere desire to dispel the confusion. My words are life and bring peace.

You can have stacks of books and can search the world's rationalizations describing the mysteries and My incredible design. But these are meaningless without My spirit. They are but dead words and mumblings that contain no power and no life.

God,

Open my eyes to see You working.

Sensitize me to feel Your presence and sense You are working on my behalf.

But even more, increase my faith to know You're my Way Maker, my Miracle Worker, my Promise Keeper, my Light in the darkness.[3]

Show me who You are so I can know who I am. If I'm to be a reflection of You, give me a clear picture of You in the mirror. My true identity is only found in You. That happens when I see You and know You. If I spend all my focus and attention looking at my own reflection and my own hurts and desires, and thinking my own thoughts, then I'm not changing anything. I'm just becoming more of myself.

Amen

"Dear friends, we are already God's children,
but he has not yet shown us
what we will be like when Christ appears.
But we do know that we will be like him, for we will see him as he really is."
1 John 3:2 NLT

"Once we carried the likeness of the man of dust,
but now let us carry the likeness of the man of heaven."
1 Corinthians 15:49 TPT

81

Complete Abandon

The memories of childhood come in waves like a summer breeze that kicks up in the evening. Flashes of pictures run through my mind like a slideshow on fast forward.

If only I could go back to those times; I'd take joy in the giggles, take interest in the conversations, and take note of each person's laugh and smile.

The days are fleeting and turn quickly to weeks and months. How I relish the seasons of life that used to roll slowly by; the afternoons that dragged on as slowly as the clouds that I watched drift through the sky.

Adulting takes over with lists, and responsibilities, and jobs, and cares, and joys, and relationships, and vacations, and storms, and life. Sunrises come too soon, and sunsets don't last nearly long enough.

But tonight, I'll dream of happy days gone by, and I'll smell the old smells and take my time skipping rocks and walking to the corner store.

And tomorrow I'll awaken with renewed intention to drink in each person's expression, to listen, to laugh, and to love with complete abandon.

"Because of you, I know the path of life,
as I taste the fullness of joy in your presence.
At your right side I experience divine pleasures forevermore!"
Psalms 16:11 TPT

"Find your delight and true pleasure in Yahweh,
and he will give you what you desire the most."
Psalms 37:4 TPT

82

Seek Me First

Each day has enough trouble of its own - don't borrow trouble. Don't spend your time and energy in mental games creating scenarios and conversations that never take place. You're just creating toxic mental real estate in your brain. You're literally creating sidewalks to poisonous picnic areas where your mind sets up camp and makes you sick on a diet of muck and garbage.

> It all comes down to trust. Do I really believe that He loves me enough to come through for me? Or do I walk in fear, worrying about the details, constantly striving to work it all out, pull it all together? The opposite of fear is love. I must choose a side. The cure for anxiety: seek first His kingdom.

You concern yourself with what you will have to eat or drink. I sent My Son to the house of bread (Bethlehem) to become the bread of life. If I could get My divine Son into the very earth that He was coming to save, I can feed you.

"Jesus said to them, 'I am the bread of life; he
who comes to Me will not hunger,
And he who believes in Me will never thirst.'"
John 6:35

"Then the Lord asked him, 'What is that in your hand?'
'A shepherd's staff,' Moses replied."

Exodus 4:2 NLT

Everything you need is already given to you.

"But seek first His kingdom and His righteousness,
and all these things will be added."

Matthew 6:33

83

You do all the right things, and you say all the right words, but your heart is heavy. This heaviness is a burden that should draw you to My side, but it actually serves as a distraction and a hindrance to our intimacy. Oh, how I wish you could learn to give it to Me and cast down vain imaginations.

You are exhausted, and yet rest is elusive. Fear from every raging battle is permeating your thoughts. Reengage your mind as a filter. Recognize the enemy's arrows, capture them, and replace them with My word. What I say about you is more powerful than your own fears.

You've been caused to doubt My voice and the vision I've given you. Cling to My written Word and My promises to you. You'll see that they line up with the rhema word I've spoken to you. If it's necessary, go all the way back to the foundation: Jesus, the Chief Cornerstone. Reflect on each layer of truth that has been laid in your life and see the building blocks of faith.

Nothing is toppling over. It's all there for you to peruse and study. Like a mountain whose layers are exposed, I'll lay bare for you the bedrock and the layers of life and grace that I have established for you. Then continue with Me as we partner in laying a new strata: a strong plate with sure footing and room to move. A high place where you'll go out and come in.

*"We are destroying speculations and every lofty thing
raised up against the knowledge of God, and we are taking
every thought captive to the obedience of Christ."*
2 Corinthians 10:5

*"Blessed shall you be when you come in, and
blessed shall you be when you go out."*
Deuteronomy 28:6

*"The Lord will guard your going out and your coming in
from this time forth and forever."*
Psalms 121:8

84

Be Settled

I have a hummingbird feeder in my backyard. To be completely transparent, I'm not a very good hummingbird host. I don't always keep the food fresh. Sometimes it gets yucky, and sometimes I let it run out, and it sits empty. One morning, after refilling the feeder, I sat, waiting and hoping, and a little hummer friend showed up! I was so excited to see her come and wanted to take a photo of her enjoying the bounty.

But as I watched her, I was reminded of myself. She flew in, tested the water quickly, and then backed away. I surmised that she was checking things out, making sure the water and the atmosphere were safe for her. Sure enough, she returned for another quick drink and then scurried off. I kept thinking "the supply is there, more than you could take in. Drink!" But each time, she would only drop by, get a taste, and was gone again.

As I kept watching, I realized that she didn't rest at the feeder. As she would drink, she continued to flutter her wings in a commotion of activity. "Rest your tired wings. Here is the place that you can sit, drink in all you can hold, and trust its goodness and purity."

Occasionally as she was flying by, she would stop to sit on a nearby wire. She sat there momentarily, close to the feeder, looking at it, studying it, but not close enough to drink.

I see me in every one of the circumstances. God's supply for me is limitless, but I come by for a quick drink, a taste, a sampling of His goodness. Even as I'm there, taking in His rich food for me, I can continue in a flurry of activity, even good activity. My mind can still be racing with plans, directions, doubts, questions, implementations, rabbit trails, and lists — never ending lists. He's whispering, "Please, sweetie, just rest. I am where all of these things will be settled. Just stop flapping your wings and drink of Me.

Like my little friend, I am sometimes skittish and ready to flee at any moment. If it gets to feel like it's too much, I can back away and then decide how and when I'll go in again. At times I'll be content to sit off to the side, close enough to see and smell the holy provision, but not actually experience its life-giving power and sustenance. The word says, *"O taste and see that the Lord is good; how blessed is the man who takes refuge in him"* (Psalms 34:8).

Too often I settle for a quick drink. I walk away momentarily satisfied because I got my living word for the day, but Father is sad because He has so much more there for me. Unlike the little hummer, I can take the Feeder with me. My Feeder isn't limited by time or space. It's a perspective of constantly resting in His presence.

Take refuge in Him. Experience His constant presence and walk with Him without striving. Drink Him in and let Him nourish you fully and completely. Enter in and find rest for your weary soul.

"Then Jesus said, 'Come to me, all of you who are weary
and carry heavy burdens, and I will give you rest. Take my
yoke upon you. Let me teach you, because I am humble and
gentle at heart, and you will find rest for your souls.'"
Matthew 11:28-29 NLT

"And he said to them, 'Come away by yourselves
to a secluded place and rest a while…'"
Mark 6:31a

"And He said, 'My presence shall go with you, and I will give you rest.'"
Exodus 33:14

85

Exchange Fear for Fullness

Fear of loss is crippling My Body, My church. Many of My people have become paralyzed because of this fear. They are losing the joy of today to the perceived dread of tomorrow. This fear of loss covers all aspects and levels:

> fear of losing material things,
> fear of losing hope because of anxiety and depression,
> fear of losing loved ones,
> fear of losing control,
> fear of letting go of old hurts,
> fear of forgiving,
> fear of finally leaning into Holy Spirit and giving Me the reign of their lives.

I am good. I am faithful. I have your good at the front of My mind. Be washed in My perfect love and watch your fear go down the drain, for My perfect love casts out fear. My will and purpose for you is beautiful and lovely and healthy and useful and full of life. Stand up in My strength and exchange your fear for My fullness.

"This is my command—be strong and courageous!
Do not be afraid or discouraged.
For the Lord your God is with you wherever you go."
Joshua 1:9 NLT

"Listen to my testimony: I cried to God in my distress and he answered me.
He freed me from all my fears!"
Psalms 34:4 TPT

"For God will never give you the spirit of fear, but the Holy Spirit
who gives you mighty power, love, and self-control."
2 Timothy 1:7 TPT

86

Which One of These is Not Like the Other?

I was in a place surrounded by lush, green beauty and life; yet, as I looked around, my eye was immediately drawn to the one imperfection in the forest. One single branch that had broken off, withered, and died. I suspect it happened during a storm when it could not handle the sustained winds that came against it, and it failed. Or maybe during the previous winter, there was a buildup of ice, and it became too heavy for the branch to bear. Either way, we have this one imperfection among an entire forest.

After I noticed it and started to pay attention to the flaw, I began to look around, looking for more flaws. You know, we're like that. Once we notice something negative and start to give it our focus, we begin looking for more of the same. There were blooms on the tree just to the right, and I even thought, "Oh, that's beautiful! I'm going to come back to that in a minute and really look at that," and then continued to look for flaws. But even after searching my view, I couldn't find more flawed branches.

Did you ever play the game as a child, "Which of these is not like the other?" This branch looks like it doesn't belong anymore. My first inclination was, "That's so sad. Someone needs to cut that dead branch down." But it was not diseased, it was just something that happened in the life of that one tree. It wasn't the trunk; it wasn't the root system. It was just one branch—not even a major one!

This is like our lives. We have an entire forest of green life, but our mind is drawn to the sad imperfection. Maybe it's something from the past that happened, maybe our failure in one area, maybe we had no part in the storm, but it affected us. Maybe it's an imperfection or an area where we need to feed or water or give extra support. Maybe there's still some potential life in that branch. Maybe the Lord is leading us to lop off the dead branch so something new can grow in its place. Maybe He's wanting to leave it there as a sweet reminder of a time when He was with us in a fierce storm.

"Do not remember the former things,
or ponder the things of the past.
Listen carefully, I am about to do a new thing,
now it will spring forth;
Will you not be aware of it?
I will even put a road in the wilderness,
rivers in the desert.
The beasts of the field will honor Me,
jackals and ostriches,
because I have given waters in the wilderness
and rivers in the desert,
to give drink to My people, My chosen."
Isaiah 43:18-20 AMP

"I don't mean to say that I have already achieved these things
or that I have already reached perfection. But I
press on to possess that perfection
for which Christ Jesus first possessed me. No, dear brothers and sisters,
I have not achieved it, but I focus on this one thing:
Forgetting the past and looking forward to what lies ahead,
I press on to reach the end of the race and receive the heavenly prize
for which God, through Christ Jesus, is calling us.
Let all who are spiritually mature agree on these things.
If you disagree on some point, I believe God will make it plain to you.
But we must hold on to the progress we have already made."
Philippians 3:12-16 NLT

The New American Standard version of Philippians 3:13 says, *"forgetting the past and looking forward to what lies ahead. "*

In the Greek, the word *forgetting* means *epilanthanomai = to neglect, to no longer care for.* In other words, don't feed it; don't water it, and don't pet it and give it undue attention.

Are there times we are supposed to remember? You bet! Several times God commanded people (Jacob and Joshua) to get a rock, anoint it, and set it as a memorial to Him. We are to remember and memorialize what God has done—not where we failed or someone else fell short.

Bob Goff said, "Insecurity wants to keep track of our failures; grace doesn't even write them down."[4]

Father,

We thank You for Your grace that lifts our eyes and encourages us forward.

Empower us to let go of what lies behind as You cheer us on! We set our hearts and our minds on Your faithfulness and Your goodness!

Amen

87

Mittens

I see mittens, hands covered by mittens. These hands are eager to serve and have received an assignment, but they are hampered by the mittens. They give their best effort, diligent in each detail, but the movements are so laborious that the tasks are slow to be accomplished and require great exertion.

As the hands continue their maneuvers, it becomes obvious that the mittens are detracting from the mission of the hands. The projects have potential, but the energy required and the difficulty of movement makes the process unenjoyable. The necessary striving and the struggle take away from the venture's culmination.

An observer would quickly identify the mittens as a hindrance and recommend their removal. Why would the hands choose to embrace the covering of the mittens? Perhaps they were initially applied as protection against harsh elements, and they served their purpose well. But that season has passed, and they are no longer needed. Perhaps they provided warmth and comfort in a cold season, allowing the fingers to stay together, drawing heat from one another. Perhaps the mittens were unknowingly applied by someone else and were gradually accepted as needed. Perhaps they were put on out of ignorance or false expectation. Perhaps the mittens were used to camouflage the hands from a perceived blemish or flaw. Now the method of hiding has become a barrier to freedom and productivity.

The Lord says, *"let us strip off every weight that slows us down, especially the sin that so easily trips us up. And let us run with endurance the race God has set before us"* (Hebrews 12:1b NLT).

What are your mittens?

What is hindering you?

What is Holy Spirit calling you to throw off?

What did you fashion in your life as a means of protection that has now become an obstruction to experiencing the fullness of God in Christ?

What are you attempting to hide with a blanket of covering that observers will accept as normal?

What is your covering that has become so prevalent that you now accept its presence as a legitimate part of you?

Jesus,

I submit fully to Your lordship. I get in line with Your word and Your Spirit. I receive Your power and authority in my life. I stand under the umbrella of Your covering. Surely goodness and mercy are chasing after me. I cease my wandering and let them overtake me, filling my heart with thanksgiving and my life with joy.

Amen!

88

The earth that I've designed for you to live on is tilted on its axis. Even further, it is constantly spinning and moving. The reality is that it is only because the earth is tilted that there are various seasons. It is only by the spinning that we experience day and night.

If you were to ponder the constant movement that I have you on, you could become overwhelmed with the thought of all that is happening around you. The sheer magnitude of the earth's process that serves its purpose is almost unthinkable. If you spend your energy considering the systems and their potential for breakdown, you would become immobilized from the enormity of possibilities.

You are in a season that is uncomfortable, and you'd rather level out your footing than experience it and move through it. It is like walking through a "fun house." When you focus on the perceived irregularities, trying to scrutinize and analyze the details, the tour loses its potential allure and joy.

I am your anchor in times of uncertainty and uneasiness. I am the unmoving rock of your salvation.

It may look dark now, but My fresh mercies will come in the morning. And in My perfect timing I will turn your present situation on a dime and in your favor. Do not fear and grasp for any object that you can reach but stay connected to the Vine.

I am flipping the script; you just keep your eyes on Me, and I will provide you a sure foundation and sure footing.

> *"... He set my feet upon a rock, steadying my*
> *footsteps and establishing my path."*
> Psalms 40:2b AMP

> *"But as for me, my feet came close to stumbling, My steps had almost slipped.*
> *Nevertheless I am continually with You; You*
> *have taken hold of my right hand.*
> *With Your counsel You will guide me, And afterward receive me to glory.*
> *Whom have I in heaven but You? And besides You, I desire nothing on earth.*
> *My flesh and my heart may fail, But God is the*
> *strength of my heart and my portion forever.*
> *But as for me, the nearness of God is my good; I*
> *have made the Lord God my refuge,*
> *That I may tell of all Your works."*
> Psalms 73:2, 23-26, 28 AMP

89

Trust or Don't

We are pressed on every side. Doubt, questions, potentials for regret flood my mind. I push back with rationalizations, lofty arguments, and snippets of frustrated conversation.

My enemies, distortion and distraction, bring travail to my mind, and the enemy's desire is to move into my physical being. I recognize the unsettling symptoms in my gut and take a note of their effect on my body.

I am faced with a conundrum of our society: treat the symptom or find the root. In this instance, I know full well the source; the decision I must make to bring real, lasting, genuine peace: trust God or don't trust God?

Right now, right here in this moment, I have to choose. And then in the next moment, I'll have to choose again. And a choice is required every moment that follows.

I pull on the truth of God's word in Psalms:

"Delight yourself in the Lord; and He will give you the desires of your heart.
Commit your way to the Lord, trust also in Him, and He will do it.
He will bring forth your righteousness as the light
and your judgment as the noonday.
Rest in the Lord and wait patiently for Him; do not
fret because of him who prospers in his way,
Because of the man who carries out wicked schemes.
… But those who wait for the Lord, they will inherit the land.
But the humble will inherit the land and will delight
themselves in abundant prosperity.

The steps of a man are established by the Lord, and He delights in his way.
When he falls, he will not be hurled headlong, because
the Lord is the One who holds his hand.
Wait for the Lord and keep His way, and He
will exalt you to inherit the land..."
Psalms 37:4-7, 9 b, 11, 23-24, 34a

Ultimately, I must trust that God works all things together for good for those who love Him and are called to His purpose (Romans 8:28).

Even if doubt creeps in, questioning my decisions, I trust that God will bring good of even my mistakes or missteps.

Jesus has prepared a place for me to "ride." He's designed a seat just for me. It fits me perfectly and the stirrups are just right for me.

In His goodness, He has provided an enormously large saddle horn, a place for me to hang on. The saddle horn isn't necessary to ensure my safety. My Jesus has got a hold on me as I'm protected by His grace, but in His mercy, He's given me a handhold, a touchpoint, a place of connection. And the more I ride, the less I depend on it. The more I trust Him, the more I know that my grip is only for my own comfort. Eventually, I will ride with my hands held high, praising Him, and knowing He's got me!

90

Tap into the Living Word

When a construction worker sets a tap, he creates an opening in a pipe. If he just drills a hole in a water pipe, the water will come spilling out onto the ground. He may be able to capture some of it for use, but most of it will be poured out and lost back into the surrounding soil. But when the worker attaches a fitting and then connects it to a new line, he can direct the water and use it for his needs. Through the new line, he can send the water where it is needed. He can water his plants without drowning them; he can fill a bathtub without overflowing; he can fill a cooking pot for a meal.

We have a spiritual tap of our own; it's our faith.

> *"My child, never forget the things I have taught*
> *you. Store my commands in your heart.*
> *Then you will have healing for your body and strength for your bones."*
> Proverbs 3:1, 8 NLT

God's word will be like good medicine, healing to your wounds and easing your pains.

When we mix our faith with the living word of God, we are tapping in. Holy Spirit will open our ears of understanding and direct the word to meet our need.

The children of Israel wandered in the desert for 40 years. For over 14,000 days, God provided them with manna to eat. It was a daily provision that could only be consumed that day. God's word is our daily bread, the nourishment for each day.

Look to God's word, both the written word and the rhema (freshly spoken) word, for life. Look for His today word for you, for His fresh message that will bring healing and strength to you. Tap into it. Mix your faith with it and watch His provision flow to every area of your life.

*"For the word of God is alive and powerful. It is
sharper than the sharpest two-edged sword,
cutting between soul and spirit, between joint and marrow.
It exposes our innermost thoughts and desires."*
Hebrews 4:12 NLT

*"God has transmitted his very substance into every Scripture, for it is
God-breathed. It will empower you by its instruction and correction,
giving you the strength to take the right direction and lead you deeper
into the path of godliness. Then you will be God's servant, fully mature
and perfectly prepared to fulfill any assignment God gives you."*
2 Timothy 3:16-17 TPT

91

Be Intentional

My child, you don't consider yourself to be a contemplator, a deep thinker. But I have put within each of you, as humans in general, an ability to imagine and consider and comprehend. Contrary to your assumptions about your own inclination to ruminate and deliberate over the more complicated issues of life, I've given you the mind of Christ. You have full access to Me.

But I have also instructed you to renew your mind by staying in My word. You bear some responsibility in directing and consummating the activities of your intellect.

I am calling you to be more deliberate. I am calling you to a new level of intentionality. *"Make My joy complete by being of the same mind, maintaining the same love, united in spirit, intent on one purpose"* (Philippians 2:2). *Intent* here means *to exercise the mind* in the original Greek writing, or *to direct one's mind to a thing.*

I want you to think on purpose toward purpose. Take care what you think and how you think because your thoughts determine the course of your life. Your thoughts become physical substances in your brain. They lead to words, *"For the mouth speaks out of that which fills the heart"* (Matthew 12:34). Your words lead to actions, which lead to habits.

What you think determines your course. *"As he thinks within himself, so is he"* (Proverbs 23:7a TPT).

I am calling you to go beyond your thoughts. Allow me to direct your thoughts as you hear My voice, and then quickly respond to My word. *"So bless the Lord, all His messengers of power, for you are His mighty heroes who listen intently to the voice of His word to do it"* (Psalms 193:20 TPT).

I want you to be intentional in developing your thoughts and in choosing your direction. There have been many seasons in your life where you merely reacted to what came in front of you. Instead of living by design and purpose, your path was determined by the circumstances you were trying to skirt. Do not misunderstand, I want you to avoid pitfalls, but when you listen for My voice and follow My leading, we will move toward something great–not just away from something undesirable. You're trying to dodge holes, and I'm trying to get you somewhere.

I want you to live with increased intentionality. I weigh and examine the motives and intentions of your heart. *"People may be pure in their own eyes, but the Lord examines their motives"* (Proverbs 16:2 NLT). By your beautiful intentions you continue to do what brings pleasure to Me. It delights Me when you are intentional to follow through on My promptings, propelling you forward toward My mission for your life. Together, we will accomplish great things for My kingdom.

> *"Since we are approaching the end of all things, be intentional,*
> *purposeful, and self-controlled so that you can be given to*
> *prayer. Above all, constantly echo God's intense love for one*
> *another, for love will be a canopy over a multitude of sins."*
> 1 Peter 4:7-8 TPT

> *"...know the God of your father, and serve Him with a whole*
> *heart and a willing mind; for the Lord searches all hearts,*
> *and understands every intent of the thoughts..."*
> 1 Chronicles 28:9b

92

Fast Track

I feel like I'm on the fast track, moving ahead at warp speed. At times it feels that God is downloading so fast that I can't keep up. Other times it seems that I'm rolling down train tracks, chasing after the last car in line – reaching for the caboose. So much changes so quickly.

It seems the gate has swung wide open and new revelation is rushing in. I am so inspired, I want to write down and save each special experience, but I can get encumbered in that process. I am still learning to discern what is for me, what is for someone in particular, and what is for the Church body.

I asked God to show me the hard things, mysteries, and I'm starting to explore what that looks like. God is not hiding things from me, but He's hiding them for me; if He puts it all out there, the enemy knows His plan as well.

As I began to better identify the Father's voice, I intentionally put myself in a place to hear and learn from others who can teach and mentor me to better hear and distinguish what He is speaking to me. He is faithful to speak every time I am still and seek Him. I have known He is always speaking, but I finally have ears to hear. I will leave no stone unturned! I feel the need to focus on both His written and His freshly spoken word and be more intentional to read and study.

"Now to Him who is able to establish you according to my gospel
and the preaching of Jesus Christ, according to the revelation of the mystery
which has been kept secret for long ages past."
Romans 16:25

"...that their hearts may be encouraged, having been knit together in love,
And attaining to all the wealth that comes from
the full assurance of understanding,
Resulting in a true knowledge of God's mystery, that is, Christ Himself,
in whom are hidden all the treasures of wisdom and knowledge."
Colossians 2:2-3

93

Silence the Clutter

One day as I was sitting with the Lord, He showed me an open room with one chair in the center. Chalkboards lined each wall, and they were covered with writing. I sensed the Lord say the following:

"This is a distraction; you're paying attention to all these words, and they are keeping you from full concentration on Me. Erase the clutter and fully experience My presence!

"Multitasking is stealing your focus. You think you can accomplish more by trying to do multiple things at the same time, and sometimes that's possible. But you're paying another price for your productivity. Not only are you compromising excellence, but you're telling your brain to look in two directions at the same time.

"You won't recognize My voice when you're not fully engaged in relationship with Me. Silence the clutter and side noise and look full into My face. I am always speaking, longing to commune with you. I desire to give you meat, savory delicacies that will feed you, satisfy you, and encourage you. You seek peace and yell out to Me, 'Give it to me; give it to me; give it to me!'

"My supply is limitless! All the while, I'm standing to the side, encouraging you to simply be still and experience it.

"You are doing the tasks that you think will please Me, and those things will show you My heart and strengthen you, but they are not a substitute for My presence. Life with Me is not a checklist, but an exquisite dance.

"Silence the extraneous noise; put away the to do list; quiet your racing mind, and set it on Me. See My face and know My love for you is immeasurable. Listen intently for My voice, and I will tell you deep and wondrous mysteries."

'You will seek Me and find Me when you seek Me with all your heart.'
Jeremiah 29:13

"But seek first His kingdom and His righteousness,
and all these things will be added to you."
Matthew 6:33

94

The Shell Game

In my dream, I was on a bus loaded with people. We stopped at an area with several small wooden buildings. One building was a store, packed with things for sale, and everywhere I looked, every space was filled.

I was there just before closing time and found a couple of things I wanted to buy. I went to the checkout counter, which was cluttered with things, and I presented my items for purchase. The clerk rang them up; I paid, and she put them into a bag.

I looked around a little more and then started to leave, checking my bag to find that what I had purchased was not there. My bag contained other things I hadn't wanted (trinkets), so I took it back to the register to have the clerk correct the mistake. She seemingly put my desired items into the bag, only to later discover that they were again missing. Each time I went back to the counter, I became more confused, as the same switcheroo happened again and again.

The clutter of my surroundings contributed to my confusion. The further the situation went, the more I felt the clerk was playing a shell game with me. I thought I was getting a desired possession, but instead, the now clerk/enemy was tricking me into almost walking away with something useless. Initially I thought it was an inadvertent accident, but the longer the game wore on, the later it got, and the more desperate I grew to leave the closing store.

In thinking about the dream, I see that Jesus paid the ultimate price in order to provide the most prized possessions: salvation, healing, deliverance from destruction, and more. He gave each of us the gifts of prophecy, generosity, miracles, teaching, mercy, words of knowledge, words of wisdom, and others.

Here's the scary part. The enemy of our soul is playing a shell game with us. Jesus has given these gifts to us through the Holy Spirit. The enemy can't steal them from us, but he can confuse us. He can distract us with clutter and overstimulation. He can try to convince us that we aren't worthy of our gifts. He can come at us with so much fear and anxiety that we are frozen in place and not operating in the life-giving ministry that will set us free. He can pervert our ears and convince us that what we're hearing isn't actually the Shepherd's voice but our own, all the while knowing that when we realize we're hearing the voice of our Father, we won't be deterred any longer. When we stand in the assurance that God Himself paid it all for us and we receive every perfect gift from Him, we'll operate fully in strength of the faith He's placed in us. We'll stand with boldness and proclaim His living word. We'll lay hands on the sick and see them recover. We'll operate in words of knowledge and words of wisdom for the building up of the Body. We'll see miracles and know that God is at work.

I've come to realize that, unlike the store in my dream, I've been given authority over the one trying to pull a switcheroo on me! Jesus restored man's authority that was handed over to Satan when Adam and Eve believed him over God in the Garden of Eden (Genesis 3).

I can now call out the enemy and stop him from stealing from me! I can call his bluff and clear the shelves of my own mind to stop the confusion and see my gifts and their purpose with clarity. I can silence the extraneous noise and concentrate on hearing my Father who promises to direct the use of each gift as I pass it on to others and draw them into His perfect presence and presents.

"Teach me Your way, O Lord;
I will walk in Your truth;
Unite my heart to fear Your name."
Psalms 86:11

"...but they allow the cares of this life and the seduction of wealth
and the desires for other things to crowd out and choke the message
so that it produces nothing."
Mark 4:19 TPT

"Set your gaze on the path before you.
With fixed purpose, looking straight ahead,
ignore life's distractions."
Proverbs 4:25 TPT

"For God will never give you the spirit of fear,
but the Holy Spirit who gives you mighty power, love, and self-control."
2 Timothy 1:7 TPT

95

Y ou've allowed your *living surface* to become cluttered. Things that were once useful, and even necessary, are now outdated and in the way.

You're so accustomed to their presence in your life that you walk around them without even noticing. These things aren't necessarily bad, they are just in the way. And because they are taking up space and mental real estate, you are not wholly free to hear Me and focus on My now word and direction for you.

So clear the decks. Move things out of My way. In some cases, you'll just move these outdated things to another *room* for safekeeping until they're needed again. In other cases, you're called to be free of them completely. Listen for My instruction and together we'll put things where they belong.

"And it will be said,
'Build up, build up, clear the way.
Remove the stumbling block out of the way [of
the spiritual return] *of My people.'"*
Isaiah 57:14 AMP

"Woe to the world because of its stumbling blocks!
For it is inevitable that stumbling blocks come;
but woe to that man through whom the stumbling block comes!"
Matthew 18:7

96

Swatting!

I am wasting time and energy swatting at insects flying around me. Some come to annoy, some to inflict temporary pain with the sting of their butt, and some to be a distraction from my assignment. Each time I turn my eyes to follow their path and raise my hand to shoo them away, I am compromising, putting on hold the attention I was giving to something greater.

It's the same in the Spirit. The enemy comes with distraction and darts to turn us from our focus and compromise our purpose. His goal is always to steal, kill, and destroy. But sometimes we believers in Jesus limit our understanding of that goal to the physical realm. It is also his plan to steal our joy, kill our faith, and destroy our anointing and assignment. If the father of lies can get us to be confused in our identity, he can dissuade us from our calling. If he can distract us with extraneous noise and confusion, he can pre-empt us from receiving the seed God longs to sow into our lives (Matthew 13:21). If he can sow mistrust and perversion, he can get us to harden our hearts.

Instead of turning our focus to the enemy and his tactics, we should be aware and wise; we study the One. We remain in the presence of the One. We stay on the path of the Way. We learn the character and heart of God through relationship with Him, and then we quickly recognize the fake. We learn His voice so that another's voice will not confuse us.

> *"A stranger they simply will not follow, but will flee from him,*
> *because they do not know the voice of strangers.*
> *My sheep hear My voice, and I know them, and they follow Me."*
> John 10:5, 27

*"Brethren, I do not regard myself as having laid hold of it yet;
but one thing I do: forgetting what lies behind and
reaching forward to what lies ahead,
I press on toward the goal for the prize of the
upward call of God in Christ Jesus."*
Philippians 3:13-14

*"But now I'm afraid that just as Eve was deceived by the serpent's clever lies,
your thoughts may be corrupted and you may lose
your single-hearted devotion and pure love for Christ."*
2 Corinthians 11:3 TPT

97

Renewal and Restoration

L ord, I will wait for you; come renew my strength.

"As you rest in your sleep, I repair your cells, restore your energy, and refill your tank for a new day. Yet, you're so reluctant to express that stillness and rest in your soul, which also needs to be restored.

"Please, honey, just be. Within the activity of your endless contemplations, your fruitless arguments, and your mental wanderings, you're missing the renewal and the restoration that I want to pour into you.

"Sleep in My arms and awake with new mercies and increased grace for your life.

"I reach out to carry you and you quickly jump into My waiting arms. The transition from ground walking to My bosom is almost imperceptible. You fit so perfectly against My chest, and I know you can hear the sound of love beating for you. You settle in and rest against Me as I begin to get a rhythm to My step forward.

"Now, Child, just be. Before you begin to get squirmy, put your eyes back on Me and rest so that I can renew and restore you."

"'For I will restore you to health
And I will heal you of your wounds,' declares the Lord…'"
Jeremiah 30:17a

*"I pray that God, the source of hope, will fill
you completely with joy and peace
because you trust in him. Then you will overflow with confident hope
through the power of the Holy Spirit."*
Romans 15:13 NLT

98

Sit at His Feet

I saw feet wearing ancient sandals. I pondered and studied and looked up verses that could explain this vision.

Proverbs 25:2 AMP says, *"It is the glory of God to conceal a matter, but the glory of kings is to search out a matter."* When God shows me something, it is my pleasure to search it out. I have the opportunity to dig in and seek His face to search out the matter. I further lean in to Holy Spirit to hear Him explain and unpack His preliminary message to me. To do any less is to miss His heart for me.

Jesus is inviting me to sit at His feet, to break open my bottle of oil, to bring a sacrifice of praise, to tarry, to come with expectation, and to wait. His Spirit is stirring the waters of the deep places, a fresh wind is blowing, a refilling is at hand, a new anointing is being poured out.

He says to me,

"Cease your striving and your mental semantics; come sit at My feet and drink of all that I am pouring out on you! My shores are wide; My waters are deep; and My supply is endless. And when you rise, you will be refreshed and empowered by My Spirit!"

"I kept looking until thrones were set up, and the Ancient of Days [God] took His seat; His garment was white as snow and the hair of His head like pure wool. His throne was flames of fire; its wheels were a burning fire.

A river of fire was flowing and coming out from before Him; a thousand thousands were attending Him, and ten thousand times ten thousand were standing before Him; the court was seated, and the books were opened."

Daniel 7:9-10 AMP

"'Do not fear, for I am with you;
do not anxiously look about you, for I am your God.
I will strengthen you, surely I will help you,
surely I will uphold you with My righteous right hand.'"

Isaiah 41:10

99

His Faithfulness

We've seen Your provision before, but in this season of lack (lack of peace, lack of stability, lack of resources, lack of power, all producing a lack of confidence in You), we've lost sight of Your faithfulness. Our vision has been blurred by our circumstances; our hearing for Your voice has been drowned out by the clamor of the world; our memory of Your steadfast love has become distant and vague.

But today, I hear the sound of the abundance of rain: empowerment, refreshment, restoration, harvest.

God is about to prove Himself! God is about to show Himself faithful. He is about to confirm His word. He is, even now, opening the storehouses of heaven and about to pour out His rain of renewal and refreshing on His people. He is keeping His promises. He is making a way for you. God is doing a new thing; don't miss it!

"Trust [rely on and have confidence] in the Lord and do good;
Dwell in the land and feed [securely] on His faithfulness.
Delight yourself in the Lord,
And He will give you the desires and petitions of your heart.
Commit your way to the Lord;
Trust in Him also and He will do it.
He will make your righteousness [your pursuit of
right standing with God] like the light,
And your judgment like [the shining of] the noonday [sun].
Be still before the Lord; wait patiently for Him and entrust yourself to Him;

Do not fret [whine, agonize] because of him who prospers in his way,
Because of the man who carries out wicked schemes.
Cease from anger and abandon wrath;
Do not fret; it leads only to evil.
For those who do evil will be cut off,
But those who wait for the Lord, they will inherit the land."
Psalms 37:3-9 AMP

"The Lord is close to the brokenhearted;
he rescues those whose spirits are crushed.
The righteous person faces many troubles,
but the Lord comes to the rescue each time."
Psalms 34:18-19 NLT

100

Contentment

So much heaviness on my heart,
Goodbyes at every turn.
Urgent, imperative, far-reaching needs
That press on every side.
God, show me something
That will make this all make sense.

I sensed Him say, "There's no one thing I can show you that your mind can conceive or handle that will do that for you."

He says, "The picture is too big, too intricate, too beautiful for you to take it all in and understand the nuances of every detail. So be satisfied with the picture in front of you that I've given in the natural. Clear blue skies, colorful blooms, green, lush trees, the sound of birds calling to one another. Be content with the stillness of this moment, knowing that I am just beyond the veil, literally within arm's reach, and I am not walking away."

He says, "I am enough. My presence is enough. My grace is sufficient for you."

"Each time he said, 'My grace is all you need. My power works best in weakness.' So now I am glad to boast about my weaknesses, so that the power of Christ can work through me. That's why I take pleasure in my

weaknesses, and in the insults, hardships, persecutions, and troubles
that I suffer for Christ. For when I am weak, then I am strong."
2 Corinthians 12:9-10 NLT

"God's glory is all around me!
His wraparound presence is all I need,
for the Lord is my Savior, my hero, and my life-giving strength.
Trust only in God every moment!
Tell him all your troubles and pour out your heart-longings to him.
Believe me when I tell you—he will help you!
Pause in his presence."
Psalms 62:7-8 TPT

101

Soul Weary

When I was a child, I disliked naps. What a waste of precious daylight time that I could use playing, pretending, or merely lying in the yard watching the clouds pass overhead. The only concept of rest in my young mind was for my body to be still so it could regenerate some needed energy for the next activity. (I have since overcome this aversion to napping.)

As an adult, I have come to know all too well that it is possible to sleep but not wake rested. In a culture of information overload and fast-paced mental exertion, this elusive state of refreshment is sought after like a precious commodity. The world recommends self-care. Jesus offers this rest freely.

Jesus gave an invitation for weary people to come to Him for rest (Matthew 11:28). He spoke these words to a crowd of people just after hearing from His relative, John the Baptist, from prison. The only person on the planet who clearly understood the identity and calling of Jesus was seeking affirmation that he had gotten it right. John was nearing the end of his life, and both he and Jesus knew it. On the heels of that realization, Jesus spoke about rest.

I think Jesus was soul weary. The soul (as in spirit, soul, and body) is made up of our mind (thoughts), our will (desires), and our emotions (our feelings). Many of us are soul weary. One definition of the original Greek word for *weary* means *to grow exhausted with burdens. Heavy laden* means *to load,* even to *be over-burdened with religious ceremony.*

Jesus doesn't say, "Go practice a set of rules and traditions and you'll find real rest." He says, "Come to Me." He invites all into relationship with Him, who is gentle and humble, to find rest for our souls.

Self-care is great, but it can only offer transitory relief for our troubled souls. Hebrews 4:16 NLT says, "*So let us come boldly to the throne of our gracious God. There we will receive his mercy, and we will find grace to help us when we need it most.*" The apostle Paul earlier says, "*labor to enter the rest.*" That seems counter-intuitive. Our labor is in trusting. We purpose to lay our burdens at the feet of Jesus and then rest in our faith in Him.

May we all step into that relationship where we trust Him and freely receive the much-needed rest.

> *"Don't worry about anything; instead, pray about everything.*
> *Tell God what you need and thank Him for all He has done.*
> *Then you will experience God's peace, which*
> *exceeds anything we can understand.*
> *His peace will guard your hearts and minds as you live in Christ Jesus."*
> Philippians 4:6-7 NLT

102

Come

Here I come again,
Just like I've come before,
Hungry for Your Word of life
That always gives me more.

I've rushed to go one day
Without the bread so true.
Then here I come with empty hands
That lead straight back to you.

The world would have me think
There are options I could choose.
But a day without Your holy love
Will leave my heart to lose.

I've tried the other loves;
they could never fill the void.
There's a god-size hole inside of me
That's longing for Your joy.

So every day I'll come again,
New mercy just for me.
I'll fill my cup to run over
With the grace that flows so free.

Come and drink the waters
Flowing from His throne.
They're rich with everything from Him,
The Son, the living stone.

103

Real Freedom

You think freedom is the absence of restraint and the ability to do whatever you desire. This is a shallow and short-sided view.

Real freedom is found in Me. Not in rules or laws or should or should nots, and not in the absence of should or should nots. You'll experience My freedom when you choose to live your life in constant connection to Me. When My words become living water and bread to you, you'll begin to desire them above the temporary things and momentary pleasures.

Freedom is a person: Jesus. When your primary focus is on the thing that you want to avoid, that very thing is exerting power in your life. The thing that you want to avoid becomes the rudder directing the ship. But if you'll take your eyes off the problems or the stumbling blocks of your life and center them on Me and My presence, you'll find it possible to submit those areas to Me. When this holy alignment occurs, I will have the influence that was previously wielded by the things from which you desired freedom.

> *"Yahweh is my revelation-light*
> *and the source of my salvation.*
> *I fear no one!*
> *I'll never turn back and run, for you, Yahweh,*
> *surround and protect me."*
> Psalms 27:1 TPT

104

Precious Treasure

We bring our junk to leave at the cross, knowing that His sacrifice gives us the freedom and the right to do that.

We lay our guilt and shame there, our regret and our failings. But Jesus sees them as precious treasure. He knows our struggle and desperation to be free of the things that so easily beset us. He finds value in our meager offering. Those things that He paid for---He wants them back: sin, sickness, depression, loss, grief, pain suffering.

Bring them to the cross and leave them there.

But then take of the free gifts for which He also paid. Take forgiveness, freedom, right standing, and a new identity in Him. Take the friendship with Jesus, the sonship of the Father, and the fellowship of His Spirit.

Leave your trash and take of His treasure!

"Therefore let us [with privilege] *approach the throne of grace*
[that is, the throne of God's gracious favor]
with confidence and without fear,
so that we may receive mercy [for our failures] *and find* [His amazing] *grace*
to help in time of need [an appropriate blessing,
coming just at the right moment]."
Hebrews 4:16 AMP

"Long ago the Lord said to Israel:
'I have loved you, my people, with an everlasting love.
With unfailing love I have drawn you to myself.
I will rebuild you, my virgin Israel.
You will again be happy
and dance merrily with your tambourines.'"
Jeremiah 31:3-4 NLT

105

Taste and See

I lay out a banquet table before you full of the choicest meat and delicacies of which you've only dreamed, with fruit of every color you've never tasted. My provision fills the table, but in your shyness, you only take a small taste and try the dishes around the table's edge.

I told you, while on earth, that I had food about which none of my friends knew. My food was to do the will of Him who sent Me.

Some of the food on this banquet table is to be fully consumed, growing you up in Me. So fill your plate, your bowl, and your platter! Don't stop short. Taste and see that I am good! But then indulge in My goodness!

You, too, are fed when you do the will of the Father, communicated to you by Holy Spirit. You will experience the supernatural mystery of My very Spirit within you and speaking to you. When you respond to My Spirit in obedience, this occurrence builds you up and strengthens you from the inside out. This is how you grow in Me, as if I've spoon fed you from My very table.

We can start slowly with the easily accessible dishes around the table's edge. Reach out to the friend when I prompt you. Write the card to an old professor and express your gratitude for all you learned and received from him. Pay for someone's dinner in the drive-through window. As you enjoy My provision, we will move on to more sustenance, like praying for a stranger in public. Perhaps I'll prompt you to stretch your faith and believe for miracles or receive revelation and change the way you think about Me. You'll begin to use the gifts that I've placed within you to encourage the world around you.

But do not reach for the savory fares out of pride, nor a sense of competition; their very taste will sour in your mouth and not serve to feed you.

Choose the dishes as I direct you, and I will use them supernaturally in your life. Together, we will encounter the sweetness of relationship, the expansion of your life in Me, and the advancement of My kingdom.

"You prepare a table before me in the presence of my enemies;
You have anointed my head with oil; my cup overflows."
Psalms 23:5

"Jesus said to them, 'My food is to do the will of Him
who sent Me and to accomplish His work.'"
John 4:34

Your Mercy Endures

Lord, You are amazing! How could I begin to describe Your creativity and the vastness of Your glory? Your creation is full of the wonder of Your thoughts.

Often, we stumble through life with blinders on, not acknowledging the beauty and splendor with which You surround us that tell of Your love for us. We trample past pictures that, should we stop and appreciate, would take our breath away. We've become so accustomed to the seasons and the lush sites around us that we no longer notice their value. Looking ahead to our next agenda, we march forward with boots on the ground and a determination to get to the next thing, the next stop, or the next task on our list.

Forgive me for ignoring Your work.

You, Lord, are lush and green with life. You are colors and You are the sounds of the forest. You are the refreshing breeze that ushers in the fragrance of honeysuckle and the aroma of grace. Indeed, I taste and see that You are good (Psalms 34:8)! As I experience You, I know that Your mercy endures forever.

"Drink deeply of the pleasures of this God.
Experience for yourself the joyous mercies he gives
to all who turn to hide themselves in him."
Psalms 34:8 TPT

"Yours, O Lord, is the greatness, the power, the
glory, the victory, and the majesty.
Everything in the heavens and on earth is yours,
O Lord, and this is your kingdom.
We adore you as the one who is over all things."
1 Chronicles 29:11 NLT

107

Come Forth

You can't focus because of all the chaos in your mind. Let go of the noise. You're just repeating yourself and afraid that someone will notice.

You're trying to fly under the radar, knowing that if someone takes note of you, they will see your imperfections and flaws. You are trying to back out slowly, hoping no one will notice that you are missing. If you do not make eye contact, maybe no one will see you. You think if you keep your eyes down and your head straight forward, maybe you will be safe.

I did not call you out so that you could hide! Trust me and be a reflection of Me in this world.

Apply truth in your life like paint on a fence. You can apply it liberally, or you can smudge it on to barely leave a trace of its presence. You can paint some panels and skip over others as you desire.

Ephesians 6:14 TPT says, *"Put on truth as a belt to strengthen you to stand in triumph."* The Amplified version says, *"Stand firm and hold your ground, having tightened the wide band of truth."*

Pick up the brush! Soak it in the bucket of My love and slather it onto the pieces of your life. Don't skip out on any area of your life. But bathe every part in My truth!

"Do not fear, for I am with you; do not anxiously
look about you, for I am your God.
I will strengthen you, surely I will help you,
surely I will uphold you with my righteous right hand."
Isaiah 41:10

"Let your light shine before men in such a way
that they may see your good works,
and glorify your Father who is in heaven."
Matthew 5:16

108

Refocus

I don't really care for quiet. There is a ringing in my ears that seems to grow louder without the distraction of extraneous noise. The quieter my environment, the louder the undesirable clamor in my head. And when I acknowledge its presence, it crescendos into a roar. The solution for this troublesome scenario is simple: refocus my attention. It is my choice in how to do this.

It is often the same dilemma with our thoughts. When we turn down the noise of our surroundings or eliminate the sideline commotion, we're left with a void that is easily filled with the agitation of our flesh. Our thoughts can bombard us with negativity and fear and frustrations, and the more I listen, the louder the messages become.

How do I halt the downward spiral of this grim and unrelenting pattern? Refocus. When we leave our minds (and our lives) void and open, we are vulnerable to the whims and distractions that fly by, taking our attention and stealing our time and energy until their pattern of silliness and mindlessness pushes toward toxicity and destruction.

When I challenge myself not to think about something, that is the very thing toward which I am drawn. I believe that is what the Bible means in 1 Corinthians 15:56b NLT, *"the law gives sin its power."*

I must fill the emptied mind – not with wasteful chatter and fleeting images, but with purposeful substance. I must replace the lies that produce despair and dread with truth. Where do I find such truth? In God's word.

I refocus my attention on who He says I am in Jesus: I am *"… the righteousness of God in Him."* (2 Corinthians 5:21b). I lean into what He says about me: *"He does not withdraw what He has given, nor does He change His mind about those to whom He gives His grace or to whom He sends His call"* (Romans 11:29 AMP). I acknowledge that God loves me and chooses me. He doesn't want anyone to be lost but wants everyone to come to know Him (1 Peter 3:9).

I look to the word of God for His promises for me. If I have trusted Jesus, I have access to all the benefits in Him (Psalms 103:2). Whatever my need, I go to His word for the solution. Then I plant that truth in my heart. I write it down. I repeat it to myself (out loud when possible). I meditate on it. And when my mind is enticed to think contrary to that truth, I dig in and do it all again.

> *"You will keep in perfect peace all who trust in you,*
> *all whose thoughts are fixed on you."*
> Isaiah 26:3 NLT

And guess what? The ringing in my ears has abated, and peace has descended.

> *"Bless and affectionately praise the Lord, O my soul,*
> *And do not forget any of His benefits;*
> *Who forgives all your sins, Who heals all your*
> *diseases; Who redeems your life from the pit,*
> *Who crowns you* [lavishly] *with lovingkindness and tender*
> *mercy; Who satisfies your years with good things, So that*
> *your youth is renewed like the* [soaring] *eagle."*
> Psalms 103:2-5 AMP

109

Anticipation

What are you anticipating? A birthday? A trip? A special event? Sadly, you don't only anticipate good things to come.

Sometimes you are anticipating a negative report, a coming confrontation, or perceived trouble on the horizon. Why are you waiting for the other shoe to drop? Why do you waste your mental energy in suspicions, calculating the motives of other people?

I have designed for you a platform, but you think that you don't belong on the center of the lofty structure. You see it hover right in front of you, waiting for you to step up and onto its hub. But you lack the confidence to make the headway and seize the opportunity.

But in My mercy, I have placed a handhold along the edge. I am calling to you, "Grab on! Take hold of the provision that I've furnished for you." You're still welcome to jump on top and ride with its perspective.

But if you are not ready, then at least ride alongside and let Me encourage you and love on you, so that you'll have the strength and courage to move up. I will meet you right where you are. I will even enable you to see with increased clarity and a vision for where we are going.

I have a place for you, a seat of authority. I'll teach you to live and breathe and move from this position, even as you are grabbing on to the handhold of My grace. I am stabilizing you supernaturally, and you don't have to fear falling. We will ride together!

Follow my lead. Look for Me everywhere, and anticipate My goodness. I won't disappoint. You'll be blessed with peace of mind and the fruits of joy, patience, kindness, and goodness. The negativity will fall off you like scales from your eyes, empowering you to see opportunities and other people as I do.

*"Let all that I am praise the Lord; with my whole
heart, I will praise his holy name.
He fills my life with good things. My youth is renewed like the eagle's."*
Psalms 103:1, 5 NLT

*"Taste and see that the Lord is good. Oh, the joys
of those who take refuge in him."*
Psalms 34:8 NLT

*"Lord, how wonderful you are! You have stored up so many good
things for us, like a treasure chest heaped up and spilling over with
blessings — all for those who honor and worship you! Everybody knows
what you can do for those who turn and hide themselves in you."*
Psalms 31:19 TPT

110

Our Framework in Him

As I awoke one morning, I saw a tube within a tube. As I watched, the inside tube was pulled out from the middle of the outer tube. Once removed from the larger tube, the smaller tube was unable to stand and began to bend over at the top. Not only could it not stand alone, but it also struggled to maintain its shape and design.

I knew immediately that the larger tube was the framework for the lesser tube. As long as it stayed within the host tube, it kept its form and looked solid. It was well able to serve its purpose and, while independent and able to move and rotate within the home, it stood in the strength of the larger tube.

Our lives in Christ are like this. God provides a framework for us. His presence surrounds us, and His Word gives us a sure foundation on which to stand. We are free to move about, to stretch, to rotate in any direction, to respond to the world and circumstances around us. And we are free to step outside this framework.

Oh, we still fit inside the Host; we don't lose our place there because we've pulled away. But when we step outside His framework, we begin to lose our shape. We're not able to maintain our strength on our own, and we begin to bend and collapse onto ourselves. Our purpose becomes compromised because our own framework is incapable of sustaining us.

All the while, as believers in Christ, we've been infused with Holy Spirit who constantly woos and calls us back into alignment with our Host. This is not to lock us up or lessen us, but to grow us, to steady us, to set us up for favor, success, blessing, purpose, and life!

When we trust Jesus, we are placed into Him, our Holy Framework.

Thank you, Father, for placing us in Christ, the author and finisher of our faith. While our spirits are eternally joined with You, help us to live out our lives within You, as You protect and strengthen us, grow us, and enable us to fulfill our very calling with joy and gratitude.

111

Soul Rest

Let your mind rest. Rest for your soul: your mind, will, and emotions. You may sit and rest your body for an afternoon, but are you resting your soul? You've become soul weary, letting the cares of the world, valid though they may be, go far beyond a distraction.

When you're missing soul rest, these cares become consuming.

There is a rhythm and an art to soul rest. But it's been misplaced and forgotten in your information-hungry world. You are driven by constant stimulation. Just as a toddler starts to melt down when overstimulated, your soul suffers when overstimulated. But in feeling the effects of this lack of rest, instead of seeking the respite it needs, it yearns for diversion and returns to the very thing that created its unrest in the first place.

I'm not talking about a crisis that's come or a situation that has arisen. I'm talking about your way of living. Put down the phone, turn off the noise, sit still, and just be.

You think you have the answer to every question in a little box. "What is this? How do you do this?" The questions that really matter are the ones you ask Me. So ask. And then listen.

"Are you weary, carrying a heavy burden? Come to me. I will refresh your life,
for I am your oasis. Simply join your life with mine.
Learn my ways and you'll discover
that I'm gentle, humble, easy to please. You will
find refreshment and rest in me."
Matthew 11:28-29 TPT

"As we enter into God's faith-rest life we cease from our own works,
just as God celebrates his finished works and rests in them."
Hebrews 4:10 TPT

112

Awaken

We have valued comfort over wisdom. We have abdicated our own thoughts and decisions to the momentary relief offered by the world, a scheme of distraction and diversion. Even those close to us may unknowingly propagate a system of false peace, spreading and disseminating a vapor of satisfaction that's both fleeting and flawed.

It's like downloading an icon for an app that you expect to be useful and profitable, only to find that the link is dead; there's no substance.

But because we experience a transitory physical and mental respite, we relent, and we set ourselves at the mercy, and sometimes the control, of a conglomerate of emptiness.

We've got to wake up, get up off the massage table that's turned into an altar to our own pleasure.

Set our gaze fully and solely on Christ, the Author and Finisher of our faith. Seek Him and find real substance and sustenance.

"May everyone who knows your mercy keep putting their trust in you, for they can count on you for help no matter what. O Lord, you will never, no never, neglect those who come to you."
Psalms 9:10 TPT

"'For I know the plans I have for you,' says the Lord. 'They are plans for good and not for disaster, to give you a future and a hope. In those days when you pray, I will listen. If you look for me wholeheartedly, you will find me. I will be found by you,' says the Lord. 'I will end your

captivity and restore your fortunes. I will gather you out of the nations where I sent you and will bring you home again to your own land.'"
Jeremiah 29:11-14 NLT

"The Lord is good to those who wait for Him,
To the person who seeks Him."
Lamentations 3:25

113

Time, Time, Time!

Please hurry because there's not enough time. Talk fast so I can get more of Your word!

"Child, there's no hurry here. You're calling out for faster, sooner, earlier, later. My time is right on time. Although I don't need to mark time, as you understand it, I knew that you would. You needed a measurement, but only to see Me in it. I will use it to blow you away. When you see Me move to keep My word in years and decades – down to the day – you can't help but acknowledge My power and My sovereignty.

"Even though I don't operate on your schedule, I won't let you be late!

"I am opening doors at every turn. You think you're locked in a room with no windows or doors. You think you're in isolation. As you examine the walls, you'll find hidden doors; openings the casual observer would never see. I've set multiple doors in every wall, leading further into My presence.

"You can't go wrong. I've set you up for success. Each opportunity that you take hold of is a doorway that I've designed for you. Throw them open and watch Me. I'll lead you every step, and you'll experience life in Me."

"Wait for and confidently expect the Lord;
Be strong and let your heart take courage;
Yes, wait for and confidently expect the Lord."
Psalms 27:14 AMP

"But when the time of fulfillment had come..."
Galatians 4:4a TPT

"For there is a proper time and [appropriate] *procedure for every delight,*
Though mankind's misery and trouble lies heavily
upon him [who rebels against the king]."
Ecclesiastes 8:6 AMP

114

Pollination

One spring, I chose two hanging flowering plants, one with yellow blooms and the other with pink blooms. I hung the yellow basket on the top rung of a plant holder and the pink on the bottom rung.

One morning, I went to the patio to enjoy my flowers. To my surprise, the yellow basket (on the top) had one stem with two blooms rising above the others. To my surprise, the twin blooms were on one stem, but the blooms were different colors; one yellow and one pink. On the plant full of yellow blooms was a solitary pink bloom, standing with its twin, taller than the rest.

In my non-gardener mind, it would make more sense if the yellow bloom showed up on the pink plant, because I could easily fathom how some mysterious plant-making color material fell off into the basket below. But having the opposite happen made me curious.

Pollination. Some friendly "worker" stepped into the pink bloom at just the right time and then carried it up to the yellow-blooming plant and set off this color-swapping situation. Okay, mental problem solved. But I couldn't let it go.

"God, why am I so obsessed with this circumstance? And why does it matter?" I ruminated over the dilemma for some time, and then I heard, "This is a kingdom principle."

We as believers are pollinators. There are two kingdoms: the kingdom of God and the kingdom of this world (the kingdom of light and the kingdom of darkness.). We are called to live in the kingdom of light.

But we do not merely live in the light, we are to be light bearers. We are to carry the light, bringing its transforming power. As we interact in the world

there is an impartation that changes the color of people's lives, uncovering
and revealing how God desires to partner with us to bring beauty and delight.
And this amazing artistry draws a hurting people to His loving arms.

"For the fruit [the effect, the result] *of the Light*
consists in all goodness and righteousness and truth."
Ephesians 5:9 AMP

"For ever since the creation of the world His invisible attributes,
His eternal power and divine nature, have been
clearly seen, being understood
through His workmanship [all is creation, the
wonderful things that He has made],
so that they [who fail to believe and trust in Him]
are without excuse and without defense."
Romans 1:20 AMP

"Therefore if anyone is in Christ [that is, grafted in,
joined to Him by faith in Him as Savior],
he is a new creature [reborn and renewed by the Holy Spirit];
the old things [the previous moral and spiritual condition] *have passed away.*
Behold, new things have come [because spiritual
awakening brings a new life]."
2 Corinthians 5:17 AMP

115

Rest and Receive

y child, you do realize that my initial design for planet earth did not include rain? In its original state, on day six, a mist (fog, dew, vapor) was used to rise from the land and water the entire surface of the ground.

Eventually, the cycle of rains came upon the earth. My purpose of watering and sustaining the earth was achieved through both systems.

Despite your best efforts, you make mistakes; you sometimes sidestep My path for you. And when you find yourself in that sad state, you fear that not only My love and grace for you will diminish, but also my blessing, provision, and sustainment will begin to dry up.

I'm going to water you either way. I will make a way to get my sustenance into you. I will meet your need!

So whether it comes up from the ground like plants sprouting with a harvest for you, or down from the sky like a rain of cleansing and nourishment falling straight from heaven, I will feed you. I have not forgotten you, and I will not neglect to provide for you!

Rest and receive.

"Instead, springs came up from the ground and watered all the land."
Genesis 2:6 NLT

"I am convinced that my God will fully satisfy every need you have,
for I have seen the abundant riches of glory
revealed to me through Jesus Christ!"
Philippians 4:19 TPT

116

Wait

I see a large black pot over a fire. It is full of a thick, brown, syrupy substance. It has come to a full boil at the surface, and coming too close could result in a burn. I know that the pot's treasure will be sweet and tasty. Trying to sample its goodness too early would be painful. But if you had skipped the boiling process, the raw ingredients would never have melded together to become the masterpiece that is to come.

Don't shortchange the boil; it is creating something wonderful.

In the circumstances of your life, you feel like you have reached the boiling point. You have asked Me for a way of escape or an intervention to turn down the heat. These options would give you temporary relief, but neither of them would produce the rich grace that I have for you.

The bounty that will come from this season will be sustenance for you and others that will taste its purity. The nourishment that you share will be confirmation to you of the holy soaking that took place in your life.

So sit back and wait on My perfect timing. Submit to My design and let Me create a feast.

*"Nevertheless, do not let this one fact escape your notice, beloved,
that with the Lord one day is like a thousand years, and a thousand
years is like one day. The Lord does not delay [as though He
were unable to act] and is not slow about His promise, as some
count slowness, but is [extraordinarily] patient toward you,
not wishing for any to perish but for all to come to repentance."*
2 Peter 3:8-9 AMP

"There is a season [a time appointed] *for everything and a time for
every delight and event or purpose under heaven."* Ecclesiastes 3:1
AMP

"For the vision is yet for the appointed [future] *time
It hurries toward the goal* [of fulfillment];
it will not fail. Even though it delays, wait [patiently] *for it, Because
it will certainly come; it will not delay."*
Habakkuk 2:3 AMP

117

I AM Your Source

There is no disgrace in your fatigue. Your efforts are honorable, and your desire is to fulfill your calling and your obligations. But weariness is not a package I give you to carry. When your efforts are not drawing from Me as your source, you will become weary.

I am not condemning you but reminding you. When you cast your cares onto Me and lean in, depending on my full supply to enable and sustain you, your burden becomes lighter, and your efforts produce an outcome that you could never accomplish on your own.

Partner with Me. Get hooked up with Me. My yoke is easy!

A yoke with Me is actually balance, a union with Me that balances the power of My presence with the potential that you bring to every assignment. Even in the natural world, you can appreciate the multiplication of effort: one draft horse can pull 8,000 pounds, but two yoked together can pull 24,000 pounds! Even better, when those same horses know each other and are trained to work together, they can pull up to 32,000 pounds.[5]

This is just a preview of our possibilities! I'm ready to raise the curtain and reveal to you how beautiful the balance of our diligent and directed work will be. Your first task is to come to the end of your personal striving and join yourself to Me. Find your comfortable place right next to Me and you'll find that the connection is fitted perfectly for you.

"For My yoke is easy and My burden is light."
Matthew 11:30

"Cast your burden upon the Lord and He will sustain you;
He will never allow the righteous to be shaken."
Psalms 55:22

"…casting all your anxiety on Him, because He cares for you."
1 Peter 5:7

118

Peace Thieves

Everywhere you look there are peace thieves: people and situations that blow into your circle, your sphere, your environment, and spray you down with their gunk.

Sometimes their stuff is legitimately your concern. But often times, they just need to release it on to someone else because they don't know what to do with it. Many times, they aren't looking for resolution, but a dump station.

Your dilemma comes in being someone else's dump station.

It takes some discernment to distinguish when Holy Spirit is leading a person to us. If so, He will fill our mouth with Godly counsel, the individual will receive it (or not), and we will both move on.

But it also takes discernment to understand when we are someone else's dump station. In this case, the individual isn't looking for resolution, but relief. Once they've sprayed us down with the junk that has burdened or troubled them, they experience a temporary reprieve from the mounting pressure against their blow valve. They've just transferred their load into our backpack.

Now we must decide what to do with it: carry it down the road, dump it onto some other unwitting soul, hand it back, or lay it at the feet of the cross.

As we serve the body of Christ, sometimes the most loving thing we can do is to direct someone in pain straight to the cross of Jesus. If we continually receive their waste, we enable and promote their sickness rather than directing them to real healing that only Holy Spirit can give. We weren't designed to bear the load, but to be yoked to the One who sees our burdens and calls us to partner with Him. *"Casting all your anxieties on Him, because He cares for you"* (1 Peter 5:7).

Whether we're carrying our own burdens, the cares and concerns of the world, or a load that someone else has transferred to us, lay it down. Release it at the feet of Jesus and then join Him in the yoke of the kingdom, for His burden is easy and His yoke is light (Matthew 11:30).

"So here's what I've learned through it all:
Leave all your cares and anxieties at the feet of the Lord,
and measureless grace will strengthen you."
Psalms 55:22 TPT

"I leave the gift of peace with you—my peace.
Not the kind of fragile peace given by the world,
but my perfect peace.
Don't yield to fear or be troubled in your hearts
—instead, be courageous!"
John 14:27 TPT

119

Atmospheric Change

How quickly the atmosphere affects you. You respond to the temperature quickly in your physical body, and even your mind and mood can be pulled in a new direction, contrary to the position and focus to which you have previously set it.

While you have received My call to set the atmosphere in worship, you have relegated it to that environment in that place: the physical church.

It's time for you to branch out, spread that calling to other areas of your life. Oh, I know you're trying, you are making an effort and wishing you could change your own mind in some areas. I am empowering you to do so.

Do not try to push through like some new age mental exercise; this is futile. It is such a balance of understanding: walking in your authority and also allowing Me to affect the difference.

But it is not a secret formula, the discovery of which will solve all of your problems. It is a walk; it is a dance with Me; it is a rhythm of leaning into Me, resting in Me while also charging ahead to take ground for the kingdom. It is an exercise in faith.

Faith - not formula - pleases Me.

Man grows comfortable in the predictable formulas of earthly living, because it is easier to memorize a list of directions or decision trees than to listen for My voice and move when I move.

You look at Me, listen for Me. Jesus explained to you that He did and said what He saw and heard from Me (John 5:19). His instruction is for you to do the same.

Together let's set the atmosphere of your life, and you can watch Me affect the change in the circumstances around you.

"So Jesus explained, 'I tell you the truth, the Son can do nothing by himself.
He does only what he sees the Father doing. Whatever
the Father does, the Son also does.
For the Father loves the Son and shows him everything he is doing.'"
John 5:19-20a NLT

"For I'm not speaking as someone who is self-appointed,
but I speak by the authority of the Father himself who
sent me, and who instructed me what to say.
And I know that the Father's commands result in eternal life,
and that's why I speak the very words I've heard him speak."
John 12:49-50 TPT

120

Flash

I saw a camera flash. It was like an old-fashioned camera with a flash cube. We can look through the camera lens, but without the flash of the cube, what shows up on the record is dark and distorted. It's not until we actually take the action and push the button that we activate the light to dispel darkness and expose what is right in front of us. In reality, the flash cube was filled with oxygen in which foil or wires were burned. It could be used only one time and was too hot to touch after flashing.

How does this apply to our life?

We must stand in faith and walk in the light of Jesus to expose the reality of what is in front of us. Circumstances look ominous until we shine the light of truth and see the smoke and mirrors for what they are: shadows and lies.

Activate the flash, which is the breath of God powered by the move of Holy Spirit.

"The people who sat in darkness
have seen a great light.
And for those who lived in the land where death casts its shadow,
a light has shined."
Matthew 4:16 NLT

"God, all at once you turned on a floodlight for me!
You are the revelation-light in my darkness,
and in your brightness I can see the path ahead."
Psalms 18:28 TPT

"The light shines in the darkness,
and the darkness can never extinguish it."
John 1:5 NLT

"Then Jesus again spoke to them, saying, 'I am the Light of the world;
he who follows Me will not walk in the darkness,
but will have the Light of life.'"
John 8:12

121

Tethered to Me

You are concerned about many things. Your concerns are trying to manifest in your body. In the pipeline of spirit – soul – body, you are flowing in the wrong direction. Things in your soul are moving into your body instead of coming from the spirit. Reverse the direction! Push the soulish issues back to the spirit. Let Me wash your soul with the water of the word. Cast your cares on Me, for I care for you.

If you know I care for you, trust that I am working it all together for you. Partner with Me, and as we are hitched together, we won't pull 50/50. Sometimes I'll pull 100% and you'll glide along with ease. But stay bound to Me, tied to Me as a tether, in agreement with Me.

Trust Me. You are hearing Me. Do not let the chaos around you confuse you or convince you that what you are hearing surely cannot be Me. I hear your wondering: "Can it be that simple?" Yes, it can. Just watch and listen. I am always good, and I do not change. Know My nature and listen for My voice. I won't contradict Myself.

"Now to Him who is able to do far more abundantly
beyond all that we ask or think,
according to the power that works within us."
Ephesians 3:20

"Set your mind and keep focused habitually on
the things above [the heavenly things],
not on things that are on the earth [which have only temporal value]."
Colossians 3:2 AMP

"When I screamed out, "Lord, I'm doomed!"
your fiery love was stirred, and you raced to my rescue.
Whenever my busy thoughts were out of control,
the soothing comfort of your presence
calmed me down and overwhelmed me with delight."
Psalms 94:18-19 TPT

122

I am restoring and replacing what's been "set aside."

You've run into roadblocks in the past that caused you to abandon a ministry, a calling, a method. It looked broken to you, and you couldn't see a way for it to be redeemed. It no longer seemed useful nor worth the effort to repair. In your eyes, it had long since served its purpose and was to be thrown away. In some cases, you didn't go to the trouble of properly disposing of it; you simply walked away from it and tried to forget its place in your life.

But the day of redemption has come for that "thing." I'm breathing new life into old methods. I'm bringing new growth to the seed that was sown long ago. I'm putting new wheels on your childhood scooter, reminding you of that long-forsaken dream!

I've masterfully endowed you with unique talents that even you don't recognize. Your flair for drawing people in, your knack for being in the right place at the right time, and the unusual bent of your personality toward what the world calls unlovable are not casual attributes of your disposition, but grand designs to point you toward an unseen mission.

There is yet an unfulfilled assignment that awaits your direction and contribution.

You'll find this "thing" in the most unlikely place. Where it sits now is not the "room" it was made for, and it is clear upon finding that it doesn't belong there. It's like a horse in a garage or a car in a barn.

Even now as I direct attention toward the "thing," some will immediately identify it in their lives; they know right where they left it and can easily find it. Others are already anxious and afraid of what else will be revealed in the unveiling of the "thing." Some stomachs are churning in anticipation, and others have just awakened to an excitement of what is to come.

But the quest for discovery is not for you. You're not meant to strain and push in an endeavor to find and accomplish this "thing" of redemption. Unless you partner with me, there'll be no lasting fruit for your efforts. You'll expend needless energy, and the result will be frustration and regret.

Don't spend your efforts cleaning out closets looking for a trinket on which to focus. Wait for Me! Work with Me, and I'll supernaturally bring revelation and empowerment. I'm doing the redeeming.

Look to Me as Your singular target. Like a magnet drawn to metal, stick to Me and follow Me step for step. Without Me your "thing" has no purpose.

> Lord, open my eyes and my heart to see if there is something personally that you desire to redeem in my life. Give me the courage to pick up what You're calling and to quickly follow where You're leading. May Your kingdom and Your grand purpose be fulfilled in me.

123

In the Valley, He Restores

"He caused me to pass all around them [bones], *and behold, there were very many* [human bones] *in the open valley; and lo, they were very dry."*
Ezekiel 37:2 AMP

You find yourself in a valley. Some valleys are places to which the Lord supernaturally leads us. Other valleys we find ourselves in as a result of our own decisions. Either way, here you are.

Some valleys are lush and green and full of life. But that is not a description of the valley where you now stand. This valley is full of bones. These bones are representative of more than bodies; they once held life and were the strength and framework for souls that have now seemingly perished. The life-giving blood and marrow have dissipated, leaving only a dry remembrance of what used to be.

But God has now called you to look. Many times, we dwell amongst tragedy that we ignore because the pain is too great or the burden too heavy to bear. But here, now, in this place and this season, God is turning your face to see. He is causing you to pass among the bones, to walk among them so close that you can distinguish the details of each one. He is taking you around about them, giving you ample opportunity to view them from differing perspectives, giving greater understanding of the scene and its varying facets.

And though the bones seem to cover the valley and are many, they all have one thing in common: lo, they are very dry. Life seems to have long ago been literally sucked out of them. The situation looks hopeless. You ask, "Why would God confront me with the things surrounding me that are so dreadful, heartbreaking, useless, and irredeemable?" Seeing it all laid out before you leaves you despairing and despondent.

But God speaks, in the middle of the spectacle, a question that introduces the possibility of complete restoration: "Can these bones live?" What once looked impossible now has a ray of light shining down on it! Could life come again in this valley?

He then empowers you to prophesy to the bones, prophesy to the breath! He gives you His very word and the authority to speak it, and with it, life is restored where before there had been only regret and anguish. This new life beats with the heart of a warrior, one who is strong in the Lord in the power of His might. See them even now as they join together to stand for unity and freedom in this new season of redemption!

Taste and see that the Lord is good! For He has done great and mighty things among us!

The bones of dreams long since dreamed are coming to life. The bones of callings and anointings are coming together in purpose and direction. The bones of hope and healing are again flowing with the life-giving blood of promise. The bones of destiny and identity are rattling together. Prophesy now! Prophesy to the breath of God to fill these, bringing life.

He calls you to prophesy! He empowers you! He has filled you with His spirit and His authority. He now stands beside you and beckons you, "Prophesy to the dreams; prophesy to your calling! Prophesy to your healing and to your identity! Prophesy, and watch the life flow."

"Again he said to me, 'Prophesy to these bones and say to them,
"O dry bones, hear the word of the Lord."'"
Ezekiel 37:4 AMP

"Then He said to me, 'Prophesy to the breath,
son of man, and say to the breath,
"Thus says the Lord God, 'Come from the four winds,
O breath, and breathe on these slain, that they may live.'"'"
Ezekiel 37:9 AMP

*"Therefore prophesy and say to them, 'Thus says the Lord God,
"Behold, I will open your graves and make you come up out of your graves,
My people; and I will bring you* [back home] *to the land of Israel."""*
Ezekiel 37:12 AMP

124

Drop the Rope

~~~

You've been waterskiing in the spirit. You've been pulled behind a boat of religion. The driver has been pulling you all around the lake, going where he desired. He's been dragging you, with water splashing up in your eyes, sometimes to the point that your vision has been compromised. You've been on a short rope, unable to maneuver inside and outside of the boat's wake.

I'm calling you to drop the rope! It doesn't make sense to you. You assume that by dropping the rope, you'll slowly sink into the water.

But I'm doing the supernatural. You'll not only continue to glide above the surface of the water; you'll have the unique ability to maneuver above waves and over the glasslike smoothness in beautiful coves. You'll follow My lead and go to places that religion never took you. Together we will experience the rush of gliding through the water, cutting a trail over it. We'll move with complete freedom - not for freedom's sake - but for the sake of showing everyone on the lake how I want to join them as well.

Our unity and our joy will lead others to drop the rope and join in our great ride.

"But now that we have been fully released from the power of the law,
we are dead to what once controlled us. And our lives are no longer motivated
by the obsolete way of following the written code,
~~~

so that now we may serve God
by living in the freshness of a new life in the power of the Holy Spirit."
Romans 7:6 TPT

"Now may God, the fountain of hope, fill you to overflowing
with uncontainable joy and perfect peace as you trust in him.
And may the power of the Holy Spirit continually surround your life
with his super-abundance until you radiate with hope!"
Romans 15:13 TPT

125

Rise Up!

There is a shaking. You initially experience a trembling. It's only slight, but you know it's there. You can't deny its presence. But hang on, My Child, it's building.

There's a rumble under the surface. You feel its power long before you see its effects.

There's a bed of stone of all different sizes, all smooth as though they've been washed over by water for thousands of years. This bed of stones has been covered by sand, mud, gravel, and pebbles, hidden under a layer of protective covering. But as the trembling increases, the covering is filtered down. Pebbles fall into the cracks of the stones. Sand, gravel, and mud are swallowed up in the smooth stones, leaving only the large stones visible. These are living stones: My people.

I am exposing My people. This exposure is not for their harm or embarrassment, but rather to expose their calling, their purpose, and their gifting. In their time under the protective coating, I preserved them, I grew them, and I strengthened them. But now they are rising to the top! Their gifts are making room for them. Their purpose in this season is being revealed, and they are stepping into their high calling.

Rise up, living stones, and take your place! Step into your holy role as you follow My presence and My lead. You were created for such a time as this!

"If you keep quiet at a time like this, deliverance
and relief for the Jews will arise
from some other place, but you and your relatives will die.
Who knows if perhaps you were made queen for just such a time as this?"
Esther 4:14 NLT

"And coming to Him as to a living stone which
has been rejected by men but is choice
and precious in the sight of God, you also, as living stones, are being built up
as a spiritual house for a holy priesthood, to offer up spiritual sacrifices
acceptable to God through Jesus Christ. For this is contained in Scripture:
'Behold, I lay in Zion a choice stone, a precious
cornerstone, and he who believes in Him
will not be disappointed. This precious value, then, is for you who believe;
but for those who disbelieve, the stone which the builders rejected,
this became the very cornerstone.'"
1 Peter 2:4-7

126

Cut the Leash

We are imprisoned by our own bad theology; the wrong beliefs that we have about God have become shackles that limit us and hold us hostage. Satan has strategically built them around our necks like a collar and attached a leash by which he pulls us in the direction he wants us to go.

The enemy began his assault by inconspicuously slipping a tiny band around our necks. It was small and hardly noticeable, so we made light of its presence and tried to ignore it.

As a candle maker repeatedly dips his product increasing its size and thickness, so has the enemy, by every lie that we have believed, dipped the band around our necks, increasing its size and thickness, until it has become a stranglehold.

We now look in the mirror of our souls to discover that the once-small band has become a wide choker. What began with "Did God really say?" has led to "God isn't for me. This is just my lot in life." Or worse, "God set me up for this misery; this is His will for me." Oh, Satan can shine it up and make it look pretty, and we can even show it off as an act of our self-will, but it is a constraint, nonetheless.

Physically we are changed to accommodate this manacle and tether. We choose to adjust, even as we are compressed and squeezed from the outside.

This neckband is ultimately connected by the most delicate links to a small leash of polished gold color. We assume that, because of the now-increased strength of the collar, the chain contains the same fortitude, but it does not. It is slight and weak but sufficient to lead us by its connection to our bond.

This very circumstance has made us vulnerable. Because of our inability or lack of understanding, we have become vulnerable to the spirits of infirmity, addiction, depression, etc. We experience the effects of these conditions in our body, our mind, and emotions, but there is a disconnect within us. We don't recognize that these maladies are a direct result of our predicament.

We have a choice to make. We can continue in this unholy state and remain harnessed to the whims of our enemy. Or we can revolt. We can stretch the link between our collar and our chain until it snaps open. The enemy has already been defeated, but he is the lawless one, lying to convince us that he still has power and authority over us. The truth is that he has no legal authority over us, and the only power he has is what we allow him.

Disconnection is only step one. Next, we must dismantle the lies. It is only by identifying our beliefs and then holding them up to the standard of God's Word that we can realign our thinking. Taking every thought captive is tedious work but necessary in this process. It is by being open to true repentance, changing our minds and thinking differently, that we snap open the choker of misunderstanding and begin to breathe freely.

Then we take our place on the Rock, the Sure Foundation. We rebuild the ancient ruins one Stone at a time, careful to let Holy Spirit lead us into all Truth.

"Therefore, since we have so great a cloud of witnesses surrounding us,
let us also lay aside every encumbrance and the
sin which so easily entangles us,
and let us run with endurance the race that is set before us."
Hebrews 12:1

"Yes, God raised Jesus to life! And since God's
Spirit of Resurrection lives in you,
he will also raise your dying body to life by the
same Spirit that breathes life into you!"
Romans 8:11 TPT

127

Vision

The mind races with resolute goal,
But thoughts tumble backward toward a deep hole.

Chaos ensues and images flash;
Memories are awakened from a long-distant past.

Some are real and some make-believe;
Some are harvests from long-sown seeds.

And just before my heart gives way
A light breaks forth with penetrating ray!

A voice calls out with the sweetest allure
Bringing me back to a calling that's pure.

He covers my heart with comfort and peace.
I lean toward Him with the greatest of ease.

My mind is renewed and finally set free
A new world of color I'm now able to see.

I've set my sights on His purpose and vision
Following His lead is now my mission.

So I'll keep my head forward and watch for His sign
As we walk hand in hand new mercies to find.

128

Nothing to Prove

Y ou have nothing to prove.

I will speak to you because I love you.

I will use you because I have put giftings and anointing in you.

I have designed works for you, special assignments that are just yours. These are tailored for your personality, your talents, and your experience in My presence. I won't leave you to accomplish them without Me. I will show you, enable you, empower you, and come alongside you to complete the assignments.

You are to do the things I've designed for you from a place of identity, not in order to gain identity! These aren't for your personal checklist but to further My kingdom. I include you because it gives Me pleasure to join with you and partner with you.

"Dear friends, you always followed my instructions when I was with you.
And now that I am away, it is even more important. Work hard
to show the results of your salvation, obeying
God with deep reverence and fear.
For God is working in you, giving you the desire
and the power to do what pleases him."
Philippians 2:12-13 NLT

*"We are coworkers with God and you are God's
cultivated garden, the house he is building."*
1 Corinthians 3:9 TPT

*"The master was full of praise. 'Well done, my good and faithful servant.
You have been faithful in handling this small amount,
so now I will give you many more responsibilities.
Let's celebrate together!'"*
Matthew 25:21 NLT

My True Identity

Someone attempted to steal my identity. There was an unauthorized transaction and, later in the day, someone made a phone call pretending to be me for the purpose of accessing my account.

I learned of this attempted hi-jack when I got locked out of my own account. Later that day, after a lot of wasted time and energy dealing with this issue, I wrote the words, "Someone attempted to steal my identity." As soon as I said them, the Lord said, "The enemy has been trying to do that to my people since the garden!"

You see, as a believer of Messiah Jesus, my true identity is found in Him. I am who He says I am. I'm not a reflection of what the world sees or says I am. I'm not the circumstances in which I find myself. I'm not the condition that I find my flesh in at any given moment. I'm not the feelings and emotions that waiver with the changing tides.

I am all that God says.
I am the righteousness of God in Christ Jesus.
I am a daughter of the king.
I am the beloved of God.
I am an overcomer.
I am the head and not the tail.
I am above and not beneath.

Just as my experience in the natural, when the enemy comes to steal from us, sometimes it will be through an unauthorized transaction. Maybe things will happen that we never agreed to, but those things are chipping away at our identity, stealing pieces of who we are.

In my case, there was a charge and then an immediate credit. Almost like a test and then a take back. This was a sign that something was up; an enemy was at work. Except for my protocol of a notification for each charge, this would have gone unnoticed for weeks. But because of those procedures, I got a red flag. That doesn't mean that I jumped on it, but I was warned.

I believe there are warnings in the spirit for us as well; some we see, and some go unnoticed.

Later that same day, a person made the aforementioned phone call. This individual knew key information about me.

The enemy knows things about us. He has watched us throughout our lives, and he has information about us. He always tries to use what he knows against us; he has goals: to steal, kill, and destroy.

Now just when we think we are sinking, we need to remember that we are protected. There are procedures in place for our benefit. As this individual attempted to gain access to my account, the institution sent out a security code. This code came to me – not the enemy. Without the security code, this person was denied access.

As I sat in church, I got a text with the security code. As I was in God's house, the enemy was at work against me. We may be in what we believe is the right place, doing what we see as the right thing, but the enemy is still moving against us - even when we don't know it.

As believers, we have a security code: it's Jesus. God sent us One who grants us access to all of His kingdom. We believe and trust. He is always at work on our behalf!

A friend noted, "The enemy went after your breadbasket!"

This one thing I know: We're about to be blessed! We've sown and now we're about to reap a harvest! A tsunami of blessing and provision is heading right for us!

"I would have despaired had I not believed that
I would see the goodness of the Lord
In the land of the living.
Wait for and confidently expect the Lord;
Be strong and let your heart take courage;
Yes, wait for and confidently expect the Lord."
Psalms 27:13-14 AMP

"But you are God's chosen treasure —priests who are kings,
a spiritual "nation" set apart as God's devoted ones.
He called you out of darkness to experience his marvelous light,
and now he claims you as his very own.
He did this so that you would broadcast his
glorious wonders throughout the world."
1 Peter 2:9 TPT

"He made Him who knew no sin to be sin on our behalf,
so that we might become the righteousness of God in Him."
2 Corinthians 5:21

130

You Answer to Me

You surprised yourself by how quickly you allowed one outsider to make you doubt your call and your gifting. Not only does this errant individual not know you or anything about your ministry to the kingdom, neither does he speak on My behalf or on behalf of any member of your body.

Don't allow those who are misled, or who have no part in My truth, to distract you or cause you to question My leading in your life. You are not battling flesh and blood but powerful forces of the enemy who have perverted My word and pushed men onto a path of diversion and wasted arguments. Do not become entangled with such individuals; it is unfruitful and counterproductive.

"If possible, so far as it depends on you, be at peace with all men."
Romans 12:18

But know that you are not called by them, nor do you ultimately answer to them. You answer to Me. Don't waste precious resources such as time, energy, mental focus, and most importantly peace, trying to prove your gifting or your value.

"Who would hang earrings on a dog's ear or throw pearls in front of wild pigs?
They'll only trample them under their feet and then
turn around and tear you to pieces!"
Matthew 7:6 TPT

*"It is better to take refuge in the Lord
than to trust in people."*
Psalms 118:8 NLT

*"…but just as we have been approved by God to be entrusted with the gospel,
so we speak, not as pleasing men, but God who examines our hearts."*
1 Thessalonians 2:4

131

Strategies

The enemy is coming after us. He is a seductress. He seduces us with charm, a tactic of pushing the boundary ever so slightly, but he never stops with our "this far and no more" line. He is never satisfied to leave us on the edge of compromise; he wants us fully deep in the waters of sin. And once we are there, he will begin his tortuous accusations, "You knew better. You should never have … You'll never be clean again." These quickly morph into our own voices, and our own regret just adds to the condemnation.

When in this space, we can look back on the journey to remorse. And if we follow the trail back far enough, we will see the gates of decision that ultimately led to our downfall.

We are wise to remember that we cannot wait until we are in the throes of temptation to trust our flesh to submit to the Spirit (and even our own wisdom to flee). The battle began long before the situation in which we succumbed. It began with a thought and then a series of concessions.

Temptation usually comes in through a door that has been deliberately left open.[6]

I dreamt recently of people who were adopting baby animals; all of the animals were cute and cuddly. The thing that all the animals had in common was that they were predators. As infants, they were sweet, but they would grow up to be wolves and bears and tigers that would devour their owners. I kept asking, "Do these people not have any idea what they are bringing into their homes and exposing to their families? These animals are killers by their very nature."

We sometimes act in the same way as these adoptive parents; they were choosing "pets" that would later prey on an unsuspecting mark. We invite beliefs and habits and behaviors into our lives that initially look harmless. But as these grow, they become more hazardous. The warnings of erratic and unpredictable tendencies give way to more serious issues that are urgent and perilous.

It is incumbent on us to inspect those things that we invite into our lives. We must make decisions on deal-breakers before we enter the game. When we pre-decide what we will accept and stick to those decisions, we remove the strong feelings and ambivalent emotions from their place of influence in our choices.

I decide that no matter how innocent the kitten looks, I will not bring a lion into my home. We should study the ramifications of actions and the trails to which they lead. And by the Spirit of God, we seek guidance in making each of our decisions about what we will adopt and allow in our lives.

"For God is working in you, giving you the desire
and the power to do what pleases him."
Philippians 2:13 NLT

"… Instead, with a sensitive spirit we absorb God's
Word, which has been implanted
within our nature, for the Word of Life has power to continually deliver us."
James 1:21b TPT

"No temptation [regardless of its source] *has overtaken or enticed you that is not common to human experience* [nor is any temptation unusual or beyond human resistance]*; but God is faithful* [to His word—He is compassionate and trustworthy]*, and He will not let you be tempted beyond your ability* [to resist]*, but along with the temptation He* [has in the past and is now and] *will* [always] *provide the way out as well, so that you will be able to endure it* [without yielding, and will overcome temptation with joy]."
1 Corinthians 10:13 AMP

132

You are dragging a heavy load. Some of what you've packed is timely and okay for you to carry. But your bag has become too heavy for you.

The problem is that you never unpack the things that are resolved and no longer relevant. Instead of releasing old hurts and needs, you pile newer things on top, setting up stones of remembrance.

I'm sending you messages of peace and signals of victory, but your view is focused on your circumstances. You've looked so long at the surrounding conditions that your vision has become glazed, glossed over, blurred by your unwillingness to look away.

Like a tragedy that has captured your attention, you see what the world sees, and you find yourself unable to stop staring.

You don't want to forgive, to let go, to forget. So out of a desire to not forget, you leave the issues piled inside your bag.

I'm calling out to you to look at Me. See Me. Change your focus and watch Me change your soul.

"Jacob set up a pillar in the place where He had spoken with him, a pillar of stone, and he poured out a drink offering on it; he also poured oil on it."
Genesis 35:14

"So if the Son makes you free, you will be free indeed."
John 8:36

"No, this is the kind of fasting I want: Free those who are wrongly imprisoned; lighten the burden of those who work for you. Let the oppressed go free, and remove the chains that bind people."
Isaiah 58:6 NLT

"As for us, we have all of these great witnesses who encircle us like clouds. So we must let go of every wound that has pierced us and the sin we so easily fall into. Then we will be able to run life's marathon race with passion and determination, for the path has been already marked out before us. We look away from the natural realm and we focus our attention and expectation onto Jesus who birthed faith within us and who leads us forward into faith's perfection. His example is this: Because his heart was focused on the joy of knowing that you would be his, he endured the agony of the cross and conquered its humiliation, and now sits exalted at the right hand of the throne of God!"
Hebrews 12:1-2 TPT

Course Correction

Recently, we took a much-anticipated cruise to Alaska. Before booking, we researched and studied. In theory, it was a trip six years in the making, so we were ready to do it up big! Due to our schedules, we opted for a September voyage, the end of the Alaska season. Ultimately, we chose our departure port, our route, our visiting ports, our excursions, and even our meal schedule.

On day seven of our 10-day adventure, we got news of a change in our itinerary. Unbeknownst to us, a storm had been brewing between our current location and our home port. The weather was clear for us to continue to our next day's destination, but if we continued there as planned, we'd find ourselves in the middle of a fully developed storm on the way home. The decision had been made that we would skip day eight's port, and head home immediately.

Proverbs, 16:9 TPT says *"Within your heart you can make plans for your future, but the Lord chooses the steps you take to get there."* We were experiencing a course correction. We were disappointed, but grateful.

God quickly began to show me the spiritual applications of the current situation.

We were indeed thankful that, even as we were blissfully vacationing and disconnected from real life (as much as one can be) someone else was standing at the watch post. Habakkuk 2:1 says *"I will stand on my guard post and station myself on the rampart; and I will keep watch to see what he will speak to me."* If we will stand on our watchtower, Holy Spirit will indeed show us what He wants to say. But we must be looking and listening.

From there we began our altered course for home. We were avoiding a bigger storm, but it wasn't exactly smooth sailing. The ride home was safe, but choppy and challenging. Often this is true. We've been shown the correct route, but it's not without its difficulties. I learned a few things from this ride.

1. When things get rocky, grab onto something solid. Holding onto the people around me may bring temporary confidence, but unless we are connected to a sturdy source, we could both be falling for the floor. My something solid is The Rock. Isaiah 33:6 describes the Lord as *"the stability of your times."*

2. Keep our eyes on the horizon. Shifting seas can bring on a queasy disorientation. Keep our focus on the unmoving horizon, the goal of the journey. When we move our gaze to the wind and waves around us, we find ourselves like Peter (the disciple who briefly walked on the water in Matthew 14), quickly sinking. The waves around us are distractions; they yell loudly, but they are momentary. We must fix our eyes on Jesus, the author and perfecter of our faith (Hebrews 12:2).

3. We can't always trust our feelings. After days of rocking with the rhythm, our brain begins to adjust; this is called "getting our sea legs." The problem comes when we return to land and yet we still feel like we're on the boat. We're swaying and feel unsteady, but we're actually on dry ground. Sometimes feelings are just feelings. We don't deny their existence, but we don't make decisions based on them. Go past the feelings to the root; what is the truth?

Sometimes Holy Spirit shows me a needed correction, and I decline, and sometimes I may delay. Often times when I find myself in the middle of a storm, I can reflect and see where I missed the opportunity for change when it was revealed. But sometimes a storm is just a storm. Jesus said that in this world we will have trouble, but to be of good cheer because he has overcome the world (John 16:33). He doesn't promise that we can sidestep every storm, but He does promise to never leave us or forsake us (Deuteronomy 31:6).

For now, let's position ourselves on the watchtower to see what He will say. And we will ready ourselves to hear and respond, keeping our focus on the Rock of our salvation.

> *"The Lord is my rock, my fortress, and my savior; my God*
> *is my rock, and whom I find protection. He is my shield,*
> *the power that saves me, and my place of safety."*
> Psalms 18:2 NLT

Listen to Me

Insecurities rage. The unexpected happens, and you're thrown into a swirl of negativity. The onslaught of messages crescendos to a deafening roar, and you're no longer hearing My voice among the many clamoring for your attention.

One message of "not here" or "not now" becomes, "Well, maybe I'm not qualified" or "Am I losing this gift?" or "I guess I'm not needed" or "Is God benching me?" "Have I made a mistake and now I'm out?"

I see your heart and your love for My people. I see your desires, and I'm at work for your good - but not only for your good, but for others as well. I see the end from the beginning. I'll open the doors for you. I'll make a way where it seems there is no way. I am not walking away from you. I am not shutting off My voice from your ears. I'm not benching you. But I am strategic in My opportunities. Let Me lead.

Thank you, Jesus, that I can trust your open hand, leading me and guiding me into places that You have set up for my success. Help me to trust You more and my circumstances less. Quiet the voices so that Your voice rises above the fray.

"In You, O Lord, I have placed my trust and taken refuge..."
Psalms 31:1a AMP

"But as for me, I trust in You, O Lord,
I say, 'You are my God. My times are in Your hand...'"
Psalms 31:14-15a

135

—————

Bunker Living

Many of us live in bunkers. We know there are battles all around us, as we feel the sting of enemy arrows penetrating our flesh and our hearts.

We build safe places. We dig down into the soil of our soul, shoveling out a place that's big enough for us to fit in, deep enough for our heads to be hidden (hopefully) from the world and our enemy. We horde supplies and bring them down into our shelter, hoping to have sufficient provision to last through the current round of fighting: peace of mind, security, safety, and a covering for our heads in the hopes that it provides protection.

We create mud shelves to store our meager supplies and only pull them out when we're desperate and overcome by the need of them.

Occasionally we have the forethought to include a few arrows of our own. But our use of them when shooting blindly from our underground fort is often shooting into the wind and praying that the offensive weapon lands on the enemy.

Sadly, God has provided tanks, missiles, and cannons, but our vision is so obstructed by the fort in which we've chosen to live that we can't see them, much less use them for our benefit against an enemy that has us in his sights.

God is calling us out of our bunkers! We've been living on defense too long! He's given us all authority. He's given us authority over all the power of the enemy (Luke 10:19).

"For the weapons of our warfare are not of the flesh,
but divinely powerful for the destruction of fortresses.

We have Holy Spirit, the Word (Jesus), and our faith to fight. Isaiah said that no weapon formed against us will succeed (Isaiah 54:17). Ephesians 6 explains the armor God has given us for protection in every area of our lives, but He also gives us the sword of the Spirit, which is the word of God.

The Lord gave me a vision of a great sword hanging in the air. Then He spoke to my heart,

"You're intimidated by the sword (the word of God) because it looks intimidating. I will use it to divide spirit and soul as delicately as a surgeon uses a scalpel. Step up, take hold of your sword, and watch Me work."

My sword isn't effective if I just wave it around in my bunker. I need to get out to fight effectively. To use my sword, I know the enemy will be close, within arm's reach. This is daunting to me, as I can sense his hot breath in my face and smell his foul being. Sometimes it seems he's that close. But God! I draw my sword, and because I'm this close, God gives me insight to the direct target of its tip. His word is sharp, penetrates, piercing the enemy, and sending him flying.

He continued, "You think there's a chink in your armor. You've mistakenly believed a lie that you're not covered. There's no weak spot in your shield – your faith in Me is indeed enough. You have the measure that I've given you. I haven't left a hole to create a vulnerability for you. I'm not tricking you or disguising anything from you."

Come out of your bunker, the safe place of your own design! Come out and live in freedom. Join in the battle for which you're fully equipped and created to fight.

The One who called you is faithful, and He will do it!

"'No weapon that is formed against you will succeed;
And every tongue that rises against you in judgment you will condemn.
This [peace, righteousness, security, and triumph over opposition]
is the heritage of the servants of the Lord,
And this is their vindication from Me,' says the Lord."
Isaiah 54:17 AMP

"Therefore, put on the complete armor of God, so that you will be able to [successfully] *resist and stand your ground in the evil day* [of danger], *and having done everything* [that the crisis demands], *to stand firm* [in your place, fully prepared, immovable, victorious]. *So stand firm and hold your ground, having tightened the wide band of truth* [personal integrity, moral courage] *around your waist and having put on the breastplate of righteousness* [an upright heart], *and having strapped on your feet the gospel of peace in preparation* [to face the enemy with firm-footed stability and the readiness produced by the good news]. *Above all, lift up the* [protective] *shield of faith with which you can extinguish all the flaming arrows of the evil one. And take the helmet of salvation, and the sword of the Spirit, which is the Word of God. With all prayer and petition pray* [with specific requests] *at all times* [on every occasion and in every season] *in the Spirit, and with this in view, stay alert with all perseverance and petition* [interceding in prayer] *for all God's people."*
Ephesians 6:13-18 AMP

136

Fallow Ground

I saw a beautiful meadow filled with green grasses and flowers. Then, in an instant, I saw it turned inside out. It looked like an orange half that was turned back on itself and everything that was underneath became visible, exposed.

The soil is rich and dark and fallow; it is cultivated land that is allowed to lie idle during the growing season. This is beneficial for overall long-term sustainability of the land. It allows the land to recover while retaining moisture and disrupting pest life cycles and soil-borne pathogens by temporarily removing their hosts.

We must keep our ground soft, pliable, and moist. It is good to rest, but we cannot let our soil get dry and crusty. When it becomes dry, it will not readily receive the seed.

We sometimes equate rest with denial or rejection of everything that comes our way. In our soul we may declare, "Don't bring me anything; I'm resting. I don't want to deal with anything." This denies us the opportunity to heal in the midst of rest. Rest is actually the best environment in which to heal. Instead of pushing ourselves ahead toward a goal of productivity, we can take the season of rest to take inventory of areas in which we need to invest in care.

As we break up the hard places and turn over the ground of our hearts, let us be open to circumspection and willing to examine areas the Holy Spirit wants to address to break up the hard places that need tending and mending.

As we allow this therapeutic process, we will find ourselves more fruitful than before as we receive the seed of a new season.

"I have never called you 'servants,' because a
master doesn't confide in his servants,
and servants don't always understand what the master is doing.
But I call you my most intimate and cherished friends,
for I reveal to you everything that I've heard from my Father.
You didn't choose me, but I've chosen and commissioned you
to go into the world to bear fruit. And your fruit will last,
because whatever you ask of my Father, for my sake,
he will give it to you!"
John 15:15-16 TPT

"As long as the earth remains, there will be planting and harvest,
cold and heat, summer and winter, day and night."
Genesis 8:22 NLT

137

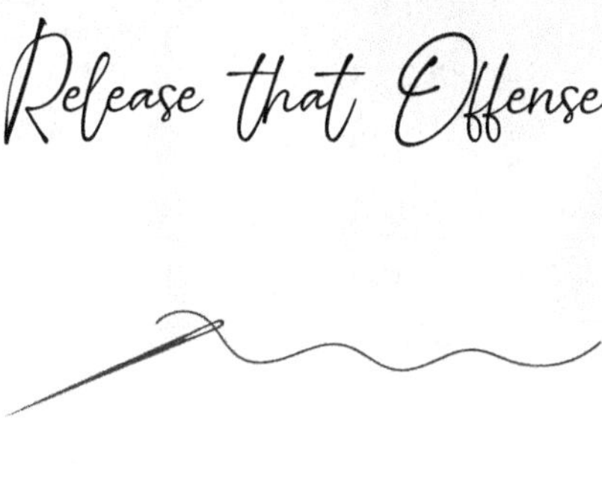

Release that Offense

LET IT GO.

You can hang on to hurt and offense for as far as your arms can reach and your hands can grasp. But the longer you hang on, the stiffer your arms grow, and the more your hands conform to the shape and size of the target of your offense.

After some time, your hands will begin to lose their feeling, and they no longer have the capacity to release on their own. Your arms have grown so heavy that they cramp, and pain creeps up and into your shoulders and back.

Now you need help. You can't let go without My Spirit and power. I was always there to help. I was standing right beside you at the instant that offense presented itself, ready to take that straight out of your hands and onto My capable shoulders. But you held on, to your own demise.

Now it will take more determination on your part to release.

Make the choice to LET IT GO.

Ask Me to empower you to release the offense and the offender. Unforgiveness only hinders you and opens the door to torture and torment.

At first it may be a moment by moment process. It is not about your feelings; it is about your choice to release. And the more you walk in this new-found freedom, the more easily you'll be able to release offense before your fingers conform to its shape.

*"Then summoning him, his lord said to him, 'You
wicked slave, I forgave you all that debt
because you pleaded with me. Should you not also
have had mercy on your fellow slave,
in the same way that I had mercy on you?' And his lord, moved with anger,
handed him over to the torturers until he should repay all that was owed him.
My heavenly Father will also do the same to you,
if each of you does not forgive his brother from your heart."*
Matthew 18:32-35

*"Tolerate the weaknesses of those in the family of faith,
forgiving one another in the same way you have
been graciously forgiven by Jesus Christ.
If you find fault with someone, release this same gift of forgiveness to them."*
Colossians 3:13 TPT

138

Produce Life

"Death and life are in the power of the tongue,
and those who love it will eat its fruit."
Proverbs 18:21

The object of the first phrase is *tongue.* In the second phrase, the object is *it*, referring back to the *tongue* (the object of the first phrase). Those who love the tongue will eat its fruit.

None of us could say we love our tongue all the time. *Love* in this verse means *love* but can also mean *to have a human appetite for something.* I may not love my tongue, but I definitely have experienced an appetite to use it. And many times, my appetite to *say* was similar to my appetite for ice cream: better left wanting.

The word *eat* in this verse means *eat, devour, consume.* At times, we've all had to consume the repercussions of our words spoken in haste or in anger. We've all experienced the regret of loose lips and saying things we only wish we could take back.

The Bible goes further in describing the fruit of words than *good* or *bad.* It says *"Death and life are in the power of the tongue"* (Proverbs 18:21a). We hold, resident within our body, the ability to produce life or death!

In his letter to Jewish believers, James describes the tongue as having the power of a rudder, a small element used by the pilot to steer a great ship (James 3:4). Sometimes we find ourselves headed down an unwanted path, consuming bitter fruit because of our inability to "tame our tongue."

James goes on to say that no human can tame the tongue. He's right. We can't, but Holy Spirit can, because all things are possible to him who believes!

"And the same with mighty ships,
though they are massive and driven by fierce winds,
yet they are steered by a tiny rudder at the direction of the person at the helm.
but the tongue is not able to be tamed.
It's a fickle, unrestrained evil that spews out words full of toxic poison!"
James 3:4, 8 TPT

"And Jesus said to him, 'If You can?' All things
are possible to him who believes."
Mark 9:23

<h1 style="text-align:center">139</h1>

<h2 style="text-align:center">Heart Bones</h2>

As I lay in bed, the words, *heart bones*, popped into my head. I reasoned this word was silly because the heart is a muscle, and it does not have bones.

The words kept nagging at me: *heart bones*. I started to dig and learned there is a condition people can get where calcifications begin to build in the heart, specifically in the valves. This calcification builds and becomes literally like bone. It has the same structure and cellular makeup as bone. Interestingly, this condition is called a hard heart.

I thought of the Bible verses about a hard heart, *"While it is said, 'Today, if you hear His voice, do not harden your hearts'"* (Hebrews 3:15a).

What does that really look like? How does someone harden one's heart? The usual suspects come to mind: sin, pride, fear, disappointments. Thinking a little deeper, many of us attend church but refuse to get caught up in being the church. Maybe we think Jesus is good for some people, but He doesn't work for us, and we're not going to get carried away with Him. This is hardening our hearts. Putting a limit on what we will let God do, or we where we will allow Him to go, or where we will choose to join in with Him are all potential circumstances of hardening our hearts.

If this condition occurs most often in the heart valves, is that significant? The valves are actually flaps that act as a one-way inlet or one-way outlet that prevent the backward flow of blood between the four chambers of the heart. In essence, they keep the blood moving forward. When they do not function properly, the heart is forced to pump with increased force in order to move the blood forward through the stiff valves.

To operate with a hard heart, we have to work harder to accomplish the normal, basic, but crucial, operations. When we live with a hard heart in any of our chambers, or areas of our life, we constrict the life-giving flow. We risk stagnation or pooling in an area. In the physical heart, this can lead to deadly consequences. When we live with a spiritual hard heart, we're compromising our ability to see, understand, hear, and remember the things of God.

He calls to us, "Today, take the limits off! Today, don't harden your heart against me! Today, let Me heal the places in your heart that have started to get scabby and crusty. Keep moving forward, keep listening, put your focus on what I show you and on listening to what I say to you!"

"Moreover, I will give you a new heart and put a new spirit within you, and I will remove the heart of stone from your flesh and give you a heart of flesh. I will put my Spirit within you and [I will] cause you to walk in My statutes, and you will keep My ordinances and do them."
Ezekiel 36:26-27 AMP

140

Learning from Missed Opportunities

Have you had one of those days where you awoke with great plans to accomplish many items on your list? You looked ahead with a sense of productivity, visualizing yourself getting it done. But at the end of the day, you looked around to see that you didn't achieve the things you'd hoped, leaving you with a sense of regret, disapproving of your own actions, or lack thereof.

I am there more often than I'd like to admit. I find myself looking back at time wasted. (Kind of a Romans 7:19 NLT feeling: *"the things I want to do, I don't, and the things I don't want to do, I find myself doing!"*). But there are a few things to consider in this circumstance. Sometimes when I see time wasted, the Lord calls it "rest." Too often we find ourselves moving and trudging ahead without the needed Selah moments: pause.

Other times we must exchange one set of duties for another. I believe many parents of little ones experience this daily. In those times, we must a) give ourselves grace, and b) evaluate the relevance and eternal value of the choices we've made.

For example, loading the dishwasher and cleaning the kitchen can take a backseat to responding to my child or being fully present with him/her to play or read or do activities together. (Not that the kitchen won't ever get cleaned, but perhaps this can happen during naptime.)

At other times, still, I must learn from opportunities missed. I must recognize my own lack of motivation, or laziness, or reluctance to just do it. In these times, I pray for the jumpstart that I need. I respond by seeing the next opportunity or available time and taking the step. I battle my own tendency to get stuck in my mind by prayer and in the spirit realm. And then I move one step forward! I begin with the most satisfying option, or the priority-one option, or the most easily accomplished option. But I move!

God does not desire that we live in regret over opportunities missed. His desire for us is life: abundant life! Abundance is not a life full of anguish, disappointment, or self-condemnation. but a life of following Holy Spirit, responding when He leads us to get onboard, and accomplishing the work He has for us.

> Thank You, Jesus, that You enable us, You empower us, You transform us from the inside. You line us up for multiple opportunities, sometimes in spite of ourselves. We put our full trust in You and Your Spirit to lead us into every good work!

"For we are His workmanship, created in Christ Jesus for good works, which God prepared beforehand so that we would walk in them."
Ephesians 2:10

"Truly, truly, I say to you, he who believes in Me, the works that I do, he will do also; and greater works than these he will do; because I go to the Father."
John 14:12

"Delight yourself in the Lord; and He will give you the desires of your heart. Commit your way to the Lord, trust also in Him, and He will do it."
Psalms 37:4-5

*"Don't just listen to the word of truth and not respond
to it, for that is the essence of self-deception.
So always let his word become like poetry written and fulfilled by your life!"*
James 1:22 TPT

141

No More Regrets

REGRET. REGRET. REGRET.

It's stealing your joy.

When most people hear the word regret, they think of big sin in peoples' lives being the number one source. And for some people, that is the case.

But your regret is much more insidious. You are wasting your energy and focus rehashing decisions. "I wish I'd done _______." "Why didn't I do _______?"

Even in those situations where you were seeking Me and made what now looks like a misstep, you are agonizing over and playing the what-if game. "If I'd done _____, then I'd be there instead of here...."

Stop looking back! You can't change what is in the past. Trust My work: I will work all things together for your good because you love Me, and I've called you for a special purpose (Romans 8:28). Stand in the truth of My complete love for you and see Me work everything together for your good. I've got your back, and I'm making up for your supposed mistakes.

Rebuke the spirits of regret and confusion and look forward. Fix your eyes on Me and My goodness and I'll put the pieces in place for you.

*"But seek first His kingdom and His righteousness,
and all these things will be added to you."*
Matthew 6:33

*"And we know that God causes all things to work together for good
to those who love God, to those who are called according to His purpose."*
Romans 8:28

142

Follow in Faith

Do you ever feel like you've wasted an opportunity? Perhaps you had high hopes for a circumstance, and you didn't follow through. Or maybe you didn't realize an opportunity was available to you until you found yourself 'at the station watching the train pull out' without you on it. You didn't realize in time that you held a ticket.

All of us have had an occasion to contemplate the moments we didn't seize, the connections we didn't appreciate, or the shots we didn't take. But what do we do with the accompanying frustration, regret, and temptation to disengage?

One priority is to evaluate the option to know if it was truly mine, is it really closed, and should I pursue it even now? Let's fight the temptation to look through rose-colored glasses, imagining everything is meant for me. Sometimes when I look deeper and search for truth, I realize that it wasn't for me at all; I just wanted to insert myself into the situation. Other times I anticipate a closed door that I know I should've walked through, when it was not closed, but closing. At that juncture, I must trust Holy Spirit for direction. Do I run through the door before it closes? It is critical in moments of desperation and high emotion that we have an ear to hear Holy Spirit clearly and follow in faith.

In situations where we know we missed it, we must lean into God, confessing to Him that we let something pass by. Then we trust that if it is something He has for us, He will bring it back around. But in the interim, we ask God, "How do I prepare and what do You need to change in me to be ready to jump on the train when it comes back into my station?"

Then we follow through, we obey, we submit to Him in the process of preparation and transformation.

And then there are those moments from which we just need to learn.

"...making the very most of your time [on earth,
recognizing and taking advantage
of each opportunity and using it with wisdom and diligence],
because the days are [filled with] *evil. Therefore,
do not be foolish and thoughtless,
but understand and firmly grasp what the will of the Lord is."*
Ephesians 5:16-17 AMP

*"For the Lord God is a sun and shield;
The Lord gives grace and glory;
No good thing does He withhold from those who walk uprightly."*
Psalms 84:11

*"Many plans are in a man's mind,
But it is the Lord's purpose for him that will stand* [be carried out]."
Proverbs 19:21 AMP

143

Take care of that to which you open your mind. Be cautious what you allow your eyes to see, for they are the lamp of your body, allowing in light and revelation. Your ears hear many things throughout the day; be careful where you incline your ears. Faith comes by hearing the word of Christ.

I gave you senses to discern what is in your physical atmosphere. But these same senses can open your mind to the reality of what is in the spiritual atmosphere. The more you protect your physical senses from negative, unhealthy, distorted, and evil influences, the better they will function in the spirit realm to give insight, vision, and discernment.

Your memory is an astounding element of your created mind. It is designed for your benefit. But it is now subject to the fall. Just as you can recall beautiful and intimate moments with Me, a smell can trigger an unpleasant memory, perhaps one you'd like to forget.

Images you've seen with your eyes remain in the bank of your mind, replaying when you desire, and sometimes when you don't. Protect your mind from the onslaught of an unwanted playlist.

"...fixing our eyes on Jesus, the author and perfecter of faith..."
Hebrews 12:2a

"Our lives are a Christ-like fragrance rising up to God."
2 Corinthians 2:15a NLT

"Your eye is like a lamp that provides light for
your body. When your eye is healthy,
your whole body is filled with light. But when your eye is unhealthy,
your whole body is filled with darkness.
And if the light you think you have is actually
darkness, how deep that darkness is!"
Matthew 6:22-23 NLT

"Faith, then, is birthed in a heart that responds
to God's anointed utterance of the Anointed One."
Romans 10:17 TPT

144

Fix Your Mind

Have you stared at something bright for too long and when you looked away, there were sunspots in your vision? Our eyes adjust to what we see, and our brains get on board with it. But when we change what we see, it takes a minute for our natural eyes and our brains to catch up.

I believe this same principle is true when we shift our focus from seeing through the lens of our soul (our mind, will, and emotions) to seeing through the lens of our Spirit (the new creature, the real us that is alive in Christ and connected to Him). What does that shift look like? It's like looking into the sun. It's like seeing light that's brighter than everything else around us. It's like taking in that light and allowing it to change us and our perspective of the world around us.

> *"God is Light, and in Him there is no darkness at all."*
> 1 John 1:5b

When we focus our gaze fully on Him, we can fix our minds on Him. When we look at Him, the light of the world, we can, by the power of the Holy Spirit, transform our thinking from a worldly perspective into the mind of Christ, which 1 Corinthians 2:16 says we have in us as believers and followers of Jesus.

When we take our eyes off of Jesus and put our focus back on our circumstances and the physical world around us, we see sunspots; our vision is distorted and there are blanks that our brains try to fill. We then find that if we only look at the darker things around us, our vision will adjust, and everything will be darker: our vision, the physical things we see, and our vision, the insight into spiritual things.

The question presents itself: I have to live in this physical world; why would I need to focus on an inexplicable, obscure, and unknowable spiritual light? Isn't it easier to just put on the sunglasses, or keep my eyes down, or look away? Yes, it's easier.

But in looking at Jesus, we can not only know Him, but He will tell us how to live and move in the darker world around us. From His light, we see the unseen and hear His voice directing our steps toward His best for us. We can walk around in the shadows, the dark, bumping into things and stepping into hazards, or we can let Him shine His light and guide us into real life.

> *"It is He who reveals the profound and hidden things;*
> *He knows what is in the darkness,*
> *And the light dwells with Him."*
> Daniel 2:22

> *"His brightness is like the sunlight;*
> *He has* [bright] *rays flashing from His hand,*
> *And there* [in the sun-like splendor] *is the hiding place of His power."*
> Habakkuk 3:4 AMP

> *"But you are a chosen race, a royal priesthood, a holy nation,*
> *a people for God's own possession,*
> *so that you may proclaim the excellencies of Him*
> *who has called you out of darkness into His marvelous light."*
> 1 Peter 2:9

145

Covering Like a Shield

We once stayed in a house on the lake in the Ozark hills. It wasn't a new house. It was not fancy, and it was not equipped with new appliances and techy gadgets. Our favorite feature about this house was its location, situated in the woods surrounded by big, tall trees. Even the top deck on the third floor was covered by tall green trees.

Covering. Sometimes that's a thing we don't realize is missing until we've had it and then it's gone.

There was almost complete shade from the hot sun all day. We ate every meal on the main deck, enjoying the beauty around us in the cool of the trees. We enjoyed squirrels and birds and a woodpecker.

At times the leaves were completely at rest, without even a stirring. At other times, the tops of the trees far above us would sway with the breeze, although the conditions around us remained calm and still.

Although the sun was bright and hot, we remained shaded and protected from the elements.

This covering made me think of the covering of God.

"He who dwells in the shelter of the Most High will remain secure and rest in the shadow of the Almighty [whose power no enemy can withstand]."
Psalms 91:1 AMP

"He who dwells in the shelter." How do I dwell there? Where is this shelter so I can rest in the shadow? If I'm in His shadow, I know I must be in alignment with Him. It's a place of positioning, under Him. To me this immediately speaks about subjection and submission.

In the Greek there are two different words for subjection. *douloo – to enslave, to bring under subjection; hupotage – submission.*

To dwell in the shelter, it is the *hupotage* definition that is relevant. I must submit myself; God is not going to enslave me into subjection. He gave us free will. When I am under *hupotage*, it is there that He will *"cover you and protect you with His pinions and under His wings you will find refuge; His faithfulness is a shield and a wall"* (Psalms 91:4 AMP).

Psalms 5:12 AMP describes the blessing of God for the righteous (in the new covenant that is all who are in Christ) by saying, *"You surround him with favor as with a shield."* In the Hebrew, favor means pleasure, delight, goodwill, and acceptance.

God covers us with His good will like a shield, a "buckler." A buckler was a small shield held by a warrior, useful in hand-to-hand combat, useful in deflecting the blow of an opponent's weapons. It also served to hide the sword hand (the offensive weapon) from view, keeping the enemy from guessing his next strike.

When we get into alignment with God, we believe what He says about us and believe we are who He says we are. We believe these things, and then we walk in them. We submit ourselves to Him and stand under His wings, His shadow, His favor, and His shield. There He provides.

> *"He spread a cloud for a covering,*
> *And fire to illumine by night."*
> Psalms 105:39

> *"I have put My words in your mouth and have covered you*
> *with the shadow of My hand, to establish the heavens, to found*
> *the earth, and to say to Zion, 'You are My people.'"*
> Isaiah 51:16

146

Don't confuse your motives with mine. You can trust My motives; they're always for your good and for My glory.

Your own motives may not always be so clear. To say that you want what I want for you can roll off your tongue easily, but you must also examine what is in your heart. Even when your desires are good and healthy and to serve Me, together we must look deeper at your motives.

Are you constantly pointing people to Me or secretly seeking their validation? Do you desire your own comfort and pleasure above My plan and purpose? In your mind, do you try to arrange things so that they line up with Me on the surface, trying to convince Me of the merits of some plan of yours?

"Girl, you'd better check yourself." Now, that's a hard word, and I realize that it is intimidating to you. But My Child, we're going places! And for you and Me to take new ground for the kingdom, it is necessary for us to go deeper, to be more intentional, and to uncover those things in you that would be a vulnerability.

As in every dimension of your life, you can trust Me as I walk you through this examination. It won't be a single event, but together, we'll make this process a way of life, peeling back another layer of your soul: your mind, will, and emotions. And as we uncover motivations that don't line up with My word and My character, My grace will empower you to release things and to shift your mindset.

Jesus,

I receive your correction and Your invitation to examine my motives. Forgive me for the manipulation in my own mind. Help me to identify impure motives and to adjust my thoughts and actions accordingly. Look deeper with me and let me be true and undiluted, transparent through and through. Lead me as we expand Your kingdom.

Amen

"Yahweh, you can scrutinize me.
Refine my heart and probe my every thought.
Put me to the test and you'll find me true."
Psalms 26:2 TPT

"God, I invite your searching gaze into my heart.
Examine me through and through;
find out everything that may be hidden within me.
Put me to the test and sift through all my anxious cares."
Psalms 139:23 TPT

"Every man's way is right in his own eyes,
But the Lord weighs and examines the hearts [of people and their motives]."
Proverbs 21:2 AMP

"So resist the temptation to pronounce premature judgment on anything
before the appointed time when all will be fully revealed.
Instead, wait until the Lord makes his appearance,
for he will bring all that is hidden in darkness to light
and unveil every secret motive of everyone's heart.
Then, when the whole truth is known, each will receive praise from God."
1 Corinthians 4:5 TPT

147

Recalibration

"But I have this against you:
you have abandoned the passionate love you had for me at the beginning."
Revelation 2:4 TPT

I operate a pool where we use an automated chemical system. This system is a valuable tool in keeping the water balanced and within optimal range. Within the system is an automatic water testing process with a constant read out of the chemical levels. How handy!

This system anticipates chemical needs. Without an automated system, we would have to test the water and react to what the conditions already are. But an automated system constantly reads levels and identifies directional trends. This allows it to respond before an actual need arises.

Within the use of the system, however, multiple times per day we have to draw a water sample and test by hand. Sometimes, the two readings will be out of sync. The automated system reading will not match the hand test. In this case, the physical test is true, and the digital readout is faulty. When this happens, recalibration is needed.

We have to re-calibrate the system. We alter the digital reading to match the physical test. In making this change immediately, we keep the system operating correctly. If we don't perform the test or follow through in making the adjustment, we will start to see symptoms of the condition: our water will be out of balance, water may begin to get cloudy, and, depending on the issue, we could begin to see the water negatively affect swimmers.

Our lives are the same! There are times that we need a recalibration. We may have good settings that are automatic in our lives, but if our hearts get out of sync, these settings will not be effective.

I must be testing against the truth. Comparing myself to other people isn't God's design. Comparing myself, even to my past, isn't testing against the truth. God instructs us to follow Him. And it is a daily walk.

Several things affect the need for recalibration in our automated process.

The way our system works is that water is constantly flowing through a test box. Inside this test box are probes that analyze the water. If flow is compromised or stopped, it will affect the readings. There must be a constant flow of water to work correctly. It is the same way in our lives. Holy Spirit is the representation of the flow of water in our lives. If we diminish His flow in our lives, our heart will pay a heavy price.

Probes get dirty, and sometimes they must be removed and cleaned. This is an easy process, requiring only common dishwashing soap. But we must have the correct cleaning solution, and we must take the time to remove the probe to clean. As people, we too must be diligent to stay clean before the Lord, confessing our faults to one another so that we may be healed. When we ignore the grime and dirt in our lives, it will build up and tarnish the lens through which we view our world. Many times, we get so accustomed to looking through smeared glass that we do not realize how badly it needs to be cleaned.

Sometimes probes fail and need to be replaced. Sometimes the measurement systems in our lives get faulty and no longer function. Sometimes the very measuring system that I'm using in my life needs to be replaced: comfort level (soul) versus peace (spirit); life being easy versus God calling me to stretch.

We recalibrate by realigning our hearts with the Father. We respond quickly to Holy Spirit and follow His leading. We examine ourselves and allow the blood of Jesus to wash us clean and get healing for our struggles. We consider our doctrines and disciplines in a willingness to allow Holy Spirit to adjust them in us. And we trust the Spirit's rule over that of our mind, will and emotions.

"Because we have these promises, dear friends, let us cleanse
ourselves from everything that can defile our body or spirit. And
let us work toward complete holiness because we fear God."
2 Corinthians 7:1 NLT

"Then on the most important day of the feast, the last day, Jesus stood and
shouted out to the crowds—'All you thirsty ones, come to me! Come to me
and drink! Believe in me so that rivers of living water will burst out from
within you, flowing from your innermost being, just like the Scripture
says!' Jesus was prophesying about the Holy Spirit that believers were being
prepared to receive. But the Holy Spirit had not yet been poured out upon
them, because Jesus had not yet been unveiled in his full splendor."
John 7:37-39 TPT

"Therefore, confess your sins to one another [your false steps, your offenses],
and pray for one another, that you may be healed and restored.
The heartfelt and persistent prayer of a righteous
man [believer] is able to accomplish much
[when put into action and made effective by God—
it is dynamic and can have tremendous power]."
James 5:16 AMP

148

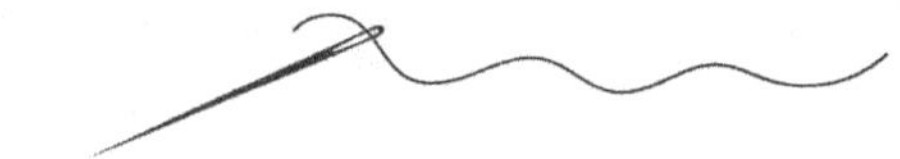

Take a full swing.

You stand in the box and look to Me for instruction on how to proceed.

You're willing to take the pitch and just watch what happens.

I know you are willing, should I ask you, to sacrifice this opportunity and bunt. You would move others forward in their positions, and that is admirable. But let Me move them in My time and for My good purpose.

I am giving you the signal to swing away. Rear back and let it fly. I've set you up with a sweet pitch that's coming right down the middle. Give it a go.

As you hear the crack of the bat, you'll experience My joy in a brand-new way. You'll not regret going for it.

> Father,
>
> There are plenty of games that I am satisfied to watch from the bench. And there are times that I am up to bat and content to take the pitch and hope to get on base with a free walk.
>
> But in my heart is a desire to swing with all the gusto of a major league hitter! Thank You for this opportunity to knock one out of the park for Your kingdom! You work through me and we will celebrate together.
>
> Amen

"Therefore, whenever we have the opportunity,
we should do good to everyone—
especially to those in the family of faith."
Galatians 6:10 NLT

"...making the very most of your time [on earth,
recognizing and taking advantage
of each opportunity and using it with wisdom and diligence],
because the days are [filled with] *evil."*
Ephesians 5:16 AMP

149

My "Yes"

s I sat down for coffee, I heard the word *"change."* This word makes sense to me. It is spring, and nature is changing rapidly. Some minor details in the way I do things are also changing. All of these things are good.

I don't particularly like change. I've heard people proclaim that "change is good." Well, good change is good, but negative change isn't really good. But here's how good God is: He promises to work all things together for our good if we love Him and are called to fulfill His designed purpose (Romans 8:28). He goes on to promise in Romans 8 that nothing can separate us from His love. So, even in not-so-good change, He will work some positive things into our lives to bring about good change.

Bill Johnson, Pastor of Bethel Church in Redding California, teaches that our "yes" opens the door for God to speak more to us. "The willingness to obey attracts revelation, because God is the steward, sowing His treasures into fertile ground – surrendered hearts."[7] God is speaking all the time; that is His nature. But my "yes" aligns my heart and my ear to hear His voice in my circumstance.

"Whenever a person turns to the Lord the veil is taken away."
2 Corinthians 3:16

Johnson explains, "One of the surest ways to increase the voice of the Lord in your life, to increase the Spirit of revelation on our lives, is to obey what you know. Obedience actually is what attracts the voice of God for fresh things."[8]

If I decide in my heart to follow His leading, I put myself in a position to better recognize and receive. We were created and designed to commune with God. When I hear His voice and yield my heart and my actions to follow His direction, it will lead to positive change.

So, in this season of change, I will declare a "yes" and get in alignment to receive! My "yes" positions me to lean in, to anticipate, to hear, and perceive better. I decide now to follow His leading, knowing and trusting that He will lead me into His best for my life and my family.

"Give ear and hear my voice, listen and hear my words."
Isaiah 28:23

"My sheep hear My voice, and I know them, and they follow Me;"
John 10:27

"Your own ears will hear him.
Right behind you a voice will say,
'This is the way you should go,'
whether to the right or to the left."
Isaiah 30:21 NLT

150

Fortified

I call you a bastion. You are a projecting part of a fortification, built at an angle to the line of a wall that allows defensive fire in several directions. You are specifically arranged to extend out from the structure of safety in order to give a wider firing range.

My word and My kingdom are your fortification. They are your defensive structure, made up of walls (or mounds) of truth around a stronghold in order to strengthen it. I, alone, am your strong tower. I am your fortress, and the one who rescues you. I am your God, your rock and strength in whom you take refuge. I am your shield and the horn of your salvation, your high tower – your stronghold (Psalms 18:2). I am your refuge and your fortress (Psalms 27:1).

As a bastion, you extend from Me. You fan out, you prolongate My fortification to provide shelter for My people during battle. Because you are in Me and a part of Me, you are a well-fortified position. Take courage that I continually strengthen and shield you. Though you see and sense the chaos and shaking outside of My fortress, I am your stronghold, and you will not be shaken (Psalms 62:6). You remain intact and are a beacon of light, drawing weary soldiers to your place of safety.

Your role as My bastion is to host the soldiers. Give them a safe place of retreat, regrouping, and preparation for the next round of fighting. *Bast* literally means *to build*. You are to build up My people. You are to love, protect, encourage, and equip My people. Teach, firmly uphold, and defend My truth. Even when the world neglects My word, dismisses it, or dispels it as myth, you hold strong the *"standard of sound words which you have heard from me, in the faith and love which are in Christ Jesus* (2 Timothy 1:13). I tell you, *"if you continue in My word, then you are truly disciples of Mine"* (John 8:31).

Instead of retreating into yourself when the battle rages, build up the fortification for My fighters. Pour into those who have come for renewal, restoration, reviving, and re-charging. Cover them with the shield of faith, protect them from the evil one by shooting with precision the fiery darts of My word.

I've given you the position and the authority from which to engage and send piercing arrows straight into the heart of the enemy, pushing him and his evil forces back. Move about on My rampart and get perspective on the strategies of the enemy. My protective wall extends for you, and I'm giving you vision and unique perception, enabling you to fight more effectively.

Don't stay holed-up in My cave of refuge. Of course, you need to visit for your own safety, renewal, and refuge, but please don't live there. My body, My church, needs you! Be a bastion in the battle to advance My kingdom.

"So now, beloved ones, stand firm, stable, and enduring. Live your lives with an unshakable confidence. We know that we prosper and excel in every season by serving the Lord, because we are assured that our union with the Lord makes our labor productive with fruit that endures."
1 Corinthians 15:58 TPT

151

Crowns

Crowns in this world indicate authority and power. When we see someone wearing a crown, we recognize that they carry an authority in their domain, their territory.

As believers in Jesus, we are given a crown of righteousness. We too have been given authority in a domain, the domain of the kingdom of God. This is our inheritance as sons and daughters of the King.

> *"In the future there is laid up for me the crown*
> *of righteousness, which the Lord,*
> *the righteous Judge, will award to me on that day; and not only to me,*
> *but also to all who have loved His appearing."*
> 2 Timothy 4:8

When we look further into this verse's meaning we find insight by exploring the original Greek meanings. *"Future"* means *"the rest of things that remain."* *"Crown"* means *"a mark of rank."* *"Righteousness"* means *"justification, right standing."* From here on, we have a rank of right standing!

1 Peter 2:9 calls us a royal priesthood. We are a holy nation, citizens with standing who proclaim the excellencies of our King.

"You spin your wheels in search of power and influence and authority in the earth. In My kingdom, you already have it! Draw your sword, the scepter of My word, and walk in your calling!

"Is the kingdom of God only something that is yet to come? No, the kingdom of God is now and yet to come, eternal. The kingdom is within you. It is the domain of the reign and rule of King Jesus."

"But you are a chosen race, a royal priesthood, a holy nation,
a people for God's own possession, so that you may proclaim the excellencies
of Him who has called you out of darkness into His marvelous light."
1 Peter 2:9

"For the kingdom of God is not eating and drinking,
but righteousness and peace and joy in the Holy Spirit."
Romans 14:17

"Jesus came and told his disciples, 'I have been given all authority in heaven
and on earth. Therefore, go and make disciples of all the nations, baptizing
them in the name of the Father and the Son and the Holy Spirit.'" Matthew
28:18-19 NLT

152

"Hey Lady, my helpie you up!"

When our son was two years old, our favorite show to watch as a family was America's Funniest Home Videos. On one of the clips, a middle-aged woman found herself in a predicament, with one foot on a boat dock and the other foot on a free-floating boat. You can imagine the scene as the boat drifted further and further from the dock, and the woman's feet moved further and further apart. Ultimately, she reached her limit and splashed into the water. As we laughed at the outcome, our toddler yelled at the television, "Hey Lady, my helpie you up!" As we saw the humor, along with the rest of America, our boy saw a need and responded with compassion.

Of course, we all understand what he did not comprehend in his young mind: there's nothing you can do for her. Today, I often see people in situations that I tell myself, "There's nothing you can do." And in the flesh, the physical circumstances, it is true that we all have limitations.

I have come to understand that there are two realms at work here: the seen and the unseen. The Bible explains that the physical reality that we can see and taste and touch is temporary. The unseen world of the spirit is eternal (2 Corinthians 4:18).

While there are needs and concerns and crises in the realm in which we live, we are often incapable of resolving these or even responding in help. This is where our connection to the unseen realm is powerful. As Believers in Jesus, we now have His very Spirit in us. Colossians 1:27b NLT says, *"And this is the secret: Christ lives in you. This gives you assurance of sharing his glory."* We can make a difference in the here and now through prayer in the unseen realm. The physical limitations that we experience on earth are mitigated by our faith. Jesus said, *"All authority has been given to me in heaven and on earth; go, therefore…"* (Matthew 28:18b – 19a)

Go in the Spirit with the authority of Jesus, praying His kingdom come to the earth and that life here would reflect the truth of heaven (Matthew 6:10).

May we all respond with compassion when we witness others in difficult circumstances and experiencing pain in this life. But let's move beyond the feelings of empathy and commiseration to battle in prayer and declare, "My helpie you up!"

"Because we don't focus our attention on what is seen, but on what is unseen.
For what is seen is temporary, but the unseen realm is eternal."
2 Corinthians 4:18 TPT

"For through him [Jesus] God created everything
in the heavenly realms and on earth.
He made the things we can see and the things we can't see –
such as thrones, kingdoms, rulers, and authorities in the unseen world.
Everything was created through him [Jesus] and for him."
Colossians 1:16 NLT

153

I Lean Into You

I'm listening for Your Word,
Draw me to the source,
Relying only on Your love
To fully lead my course.

I lean into You
And take hold of your hand,
Just the brush of Your garment
Empowers me to stand.

I've been living in a bunker
Of my own design,
But I'm coming out to fight;
I'm joining to the vine.

As soon as I lean in
And put my trust in You,
I feel Your presence steady me,
And I can see breakthrough.

Now I'm breaking free,
From the cave of my own prison,
Leaning into You I find
New life is arisen.

154

Grace upon Grace

The enemy is ramping up his assault in the earth and many are experiencing his attempts at distraction or destruction. I know you are bombarded with sensations on every side. It's like an exposed nerve that is perpetually irritated by mere air. Even good sensation becomes too much to bear when your heart is opened wide and vulnerable to every element.

But don't be deceived by him. You can quickly become so overwhelmed that you'd rather not feel at all than to be so assaulted by the sharpness and fullness of feelings. When you stand here, even in My love and the brightness of My glory, it can touch you as painful. Pain has purpose in the natural: to drive you to healing. And pain's use to you is to drive you straight to Me.

Satan is not in a battle with Me for power, for I am all powerful. He is in a battle with you. It is the original question: who will you believe?

While you are looking around in your horizontal view at circumstances and skirmishes that he designed, I am above and below at work. Just below the surface of the waters, there is a boiling of My presence that is stirring and creating a commotion of change and power that is moving toward the surface and headed toward the shores of your knowing. I am coming in wave after wave, bringing revelation, and grace upon grace, to cover and wash over you.

Stop looking for the hand of the enemy. Remove your focus from his efforts in the earth. Put your focus on My plans and My grace and My goodness. You will find what you seek!

"I will climb up to my watchtower and stand at my guard post. There I will wait to see what the Lord says and how he will answer my complaint. Then the Lord said to me, 'Write my answer plainly on tablets, so that a runner can carry the correct message to others. This vision is for a future time. It describes the end, and it will be fulfilled. If it seems slow in coming, wait patiently, for it will surely take place. It will not be delayed.'"
Habakkuk 2:1-3 NLT

"That is why I tell you not to worry about everyday life –
whether you have enough food and drink, or enough clothes to wear.
Isn't life more than food, and our body more than clothing?
Look at the birds. They don't plant or harvest or store food in barns,
for your heavenly Father feeds them.
And aren't you far more valuable to him than they are?
Can all your worries add a single moment to your life?"
Matthew 6:25-27 NLT

155

Layer upon Layer

Growing up in church, I was familiar with the tradition of communion. I understood that it was a sacrament of remembering what Jesus has done for us. That was pretty much all I experienced in it. Remembering and appreciating. And that is a lot. But not until later did I realize there is so much more.

Layer upon layer the Lord unfolded to me the realization of the much fuller opportunities in communion: taking hold of all the benefits of Jesus' sacrifice for us. I thought it was all about salvation, and it is, but that's just the opening story, the first level, the outside seal. And that would be enough, but God is so good that He does not stop there!

Initially, the last supper, Passover, was to remember how God rescued His people from bondage and oppression, how the angel of death passed over them when they applied the blood of the lamb over their door posts. And we still celebrate those two things today as believers. We apply the blood of Jesus over our lives, and we are eternally saved, rescued by grace from the enemy.

But that's not all.

You see, no one told me about the benefits. *"Bless the Lord, O my soul, and forget none of His benefits;"* Benefit of eternal salvation, okay. But there's more. *"Who pardons all your iniquities,"* (okay, I got that part), *Who heals all your diseases; Who redeems your life from the pit, Who crowns you with lovingkindness and compassion; Who satisfies your years with good things, So that your youth is renewed like the eagle"* (Psalms 103:2-5). These are now benefits--not in the sweet-by-and-by benefits. He satisfies your years and restores your youth; these are times and seasons in this life!

All of the benefits are available to me. How do I get them? Just like salvation, I simply believe and receive. There is no work on my part that makes me eligible. I could not possibly do enough good to warrant my receiving.

So when I celebrate communion, I am mixing my faith with the Word. I am receiving; I am activating all of the benefits.

In addition to understanding the benefits of Jesus' sacrifice, I now see that I have full access. We have been granted full access. I thought that communion was a church thing, a congregational activity for the body, and it is. But it is also for the body! The Body of Christ (the church) and the body of the individual (His temple).

When we come to the table (alone or with the Body), we are aligning ourselves with Christ, reconnecting to the vine, proclaiming His body and His sacrifice, both personally and corporately. We are proclaiming the reality of heaven over every area of our lives.

When I am experiencing symptoms in my body, I can take communion. When I am struggling in my mind or emotions, I can take communion. When I feel overwhelmed or at a crossroads or needing a specific word, I can take communion. Jesus said, *"I am the living bread that came down out of heaven; if anyone eats of this bread, he will live forever"* (John 6: 51a).

"While they were eating, Jesus took some bread, and after a blessing,
He broke it and gave it to the disciples, and said, 'Take, eat; this is My body.'
And when He had taken a cup and given thanks, He gave it to them, saying,
'Drink from it, all of you; for this is My blood of the covenant,
which is poured out for many for forgiveness of sins.'"
Matthew 26:26-28

"Whenever you eat this bread and drink this cup, you are retelling the story,
proclaiming our Lord's death until he comes."
1 Corinthians 11:26 TPT

156

Forward, March

I'm calling you to march! I'm calling you to walk forward in the victory that is yours.

Your steps need not be tenuous or hesitant. Stand up and walk forward. I'm leading. Like a parade, I'm setting the route and the pace. You step where I step and follow Me. Plant your feet in the imprint of My steps.

Like a great formation of warriors, you step into alignment with My will and My good purpose. You join in the great walk with brothers and sisters who march now and who've gone before. A mighty audience of witnesses lines the heavenlies with cheers of encouragement. As they call out, your steps gain in weight and stride, toward the high calling.

Don't look to the right or left but keep your focus and attention on Me. I am your lead and your rear guard.

"As a prisoner of the Lord, I plead with you to walk holy,
in a way that is suitable to your high rank,
given to you in your divine calling."
Ephesians 4:1 TPT

"I press on toward the goal for the prize of the
upward call of God in Christ Jesus."
Philippians 3:14

"As for us, we have all of these great witnesses who encircle us like clouds.
So we must let go of every wound that has pierced
us and the sin we so easily fall into.
Then we will be able to run life's marathon race
with passion and determination,
for the path has been already marked out before us."
Hebrews 12:1 TPT

157

New Revelation

We are entering a new season in the earth and a new season in the Spirit. Many of us are coming out of a trying season.

Out of a season of loneliness/isolation, anxiety, fear and dread of the future, busyness; into a season of new revelation.

God is taking what He showed us, and He is calling us to move out of that season and into a fresh move of His Spirit. We're coming into a time of new possibilities, new assignments, and new dimensions.

Get ready, get ready, get ready!

Step into God's "sanitation station" and let Him wash you with the washing of the Word, and then step out with the fullness of His power into a divine set up for His glory to be revealed in you.

"So may we never be arrogant, or look down on
another, for each of us is an original.
We must forsake all jealousy that diminishes the value of others."
Galatians 5:26 TPT

"He saved us,
resurrecting us through the washing of rebirth.
We are made completely new by the Holy Spirit,
whom he splashed over us richly
by Jesus, the Messiah, our Life Giver."
Titus 3:6 TPT

"So don't be impatient for Yahweh to act;
keep moving forward steadily in his ways,
and he will exalt you to possess the land.
You'll watch with your own eyes
and see the wicked lose everything."
Psalms 37:34 TPT

158

Lift Your Shield

Darts fly from the enemy's bow and are aimed straight at your vulnerabilities. He knows your heart and points his weapon right at your weakness.

Shore up your armor. Lift your shield and I will show you the incoming arrows. By the Spirit, I will enable you to anticipate the attack. I will give you the agility and the strategy and the energy to withstand this battle.

I'll not leave you to fight on your own. Not only will I sustain you, but I will fight for you. You need only to stand.

"Then Moses said to the people, 'Do not be afraid! Take your stand
[be firm and confident and undismayed] *and see the salvation of*
the Lord which He will accomplish for you today; for those Egyptians
whom you have seen today, you will never see again. The Lord will
fight for you while you [only need to] *keep silent and remain calm.'"*
Exodus 14:13-14 AMP

"Do not fear [anything], *for I am with you;*
Do not be afraid, for I am your God.
I will strengthen you, be assured I will help you;
I will certainly take hold of you with My righteous right hand
[a hand of justice, of power, of victory, of salvation]."
Isaiah 41:10 AMP

"In [speaking] *the word of truth, in the power of God;*
by the weapons of righteousness for the right hand
[like holding the sword to attack]
and for the left [like holding the shield to defend]."
2 Corinthians 6:7 AMP

159

Shifting Seasons

The season has shifted. You don't feel it yet. You don't realize that anything has changed, but indeed it has. There's a new reality; you just haven't seen it yet.

You've been asking me about things to come, and they are coming. You've begged Me to literally move you forward, and I am. But I'm moving everything – not just you.

Just as the earth is spinning with you on it, yet you don't feel a thing, so it is in this case.

I am moving everything around you. It's a divine set up. I could pick you up and plant you forward, but the atmosphere would not be supernaturally ready for you.

I'm at work! Continue to contend for the promises I've spoken to you.

"'For I know the plans and thoughts that I have for you,' says the Lord,
'plans for peace and well-being and not for disaster,
to give you a future and a hope.'"
Jeremiah 29:11 AMP

"Now Jabez called on the God of Israel, saying,
'Oh that You would bless me indeed
and enlarge my border, and that Your hand might be with me,
and that You would keep me from harm that it may not pain me!'
And God granted him what he requested."
1 Chronicles 4:10

160

Bring 'em Near

You've been on the ship of life, and God's current has moved you forward from one port to another. Recently, you found yourself in deep waters, knowing that God is calling you to an assignment. You are looking in every direction for its appearance, but you can't seem to find it.

A new season is here. I see you standing on the bow of the boat. You have a telescope in your hand, and as you bring it to your eye, Holy Spirit brings things into focus. He zeros in on the place that He has for you.

Now that He has given you clarity of vision, you can navigate into divine position. He is dialing down on the place He has for you. As you scan the horizon, "suddenly" it will appear, and you will recognize it!

The tool that He has given you, the telescope, was historically called "bring 'em near." Your tool is His presence! By bringing Him near, by drawing close, by beholding Him in your presence, you will allow Him to focus your vision. He is Jehovah Jireh, The God Who Sees! And the God Who will show you!

"Your ears will hear a word behind you, 'This is the way, walk in it'
whenever you turn to the right or to the left."
Isaiah 30:21

"I hear the Lord saying, 'I will stay close to you,
instructing and guiding you along the pathway for your life.
I will advise you along the way
and lead you forth with my eyes as your guide.

So don't make it difficult; don't be stubborn
when I take you where you've not been before.
Don't make me tug you and pull you along.
Just come with me!'"
Psalms 32:8-9 TPT

161

Giants Are Falling!

You are entering a season of falling giants. You hear rumbling in the distance, and you're intimidated by the sound. You can't see it yet, but giants are falling.

You'll use the weapons I've given to you but be unhindered by armor that doesn't suit you. Walk out into the open with My Word on your lips and watch as giants fall!

Thunderings of them falling will garner much attention, but this is not your focus. Keep your eyes on Me. Say what you hear Me say, and your arrows will find their target.

The enemies that you believed were untouchable will succumb. Watch Me! All the giants are falling: the giants of fear, lack, performance mentality, the fear of missing out, the memory of feelings that prevent today from being all it could be, your sad attempt at control.

Stand and see the salvation of the Lord.

"It is the same with my word.
I send it out, and it always produces fruit.
It will accomplish all I want it to,
and it will prosper everywhere I send it.
You will live in joy and peace.
The mountains and hills will burst into song,
and the trees of the field will clap their hands!

Where once there were thorns, cypress trees will grow.
Where nettles grew, myrtles will sprout up.
These events will bring great honor to the Lord's name;
they will be an everlasting sign of his power and love."
Isaiah 55:11-13 NLT

"David replied to the Philistine, 'You come to
me with sword, spear, and javelin,
but I come to you in the name of the Lord of Heaven's Armies—the God
of the armies of Israel, whom you have defied. And everyone assembled
here will know that the Lord rescues his people, but not with sword
and spear. This is the Lord's battle, and he will give you to us!'"
1 Samuel 17:45, 47 NLT

His Prism

I have worn glasses most of my life. Over the past couple of years, my eyes have started to change. (That happens to lots of people over 50!). I started to see double. When it was first noticed, my prescription changed only slightly, so I elected not to get new lenses. A few months ago, the prescription changed a little more, so I got new glasses. The prescription contains a "prism" to correct the tendency to see double. It does not change what I see, but it changes the way that I see it.

Since I did not correct it from beginning, my brain learned to compensate for the deficiency, even though it could not fully correct my vision. My new glasses are to correct the issue, but when I put them on, my brain, which is a part of my soul (my mind, my will, and my emotions) says, "This isn't right," because it seems blurry at the beginning. My brain is trying to compensate for the deficiency, and it tells me to take the glasses off, even though they can fully correct my vision. If I leave them on, my brain will adjust, and I can see clearly.

It's like that with us. As believers, there is a prism that look we through in the Spirit. It's God's word, His grace and His Love. We can choose to look through that prism and see clearly. But when we're not looking through the prism of God, our soul tries to compensate for what we see in the natural that is distorted and tries to explain it. It tells us, "Hold on; I can figure this out. You don't need to change your prism; I can figure this out." But the reality is, when we look through the prism of God, it clarifies everything we see. We can still see the same things, but our perspective is different, and the way we see is different.

To have a real clarity of vision, we can only look through the prism of God's word, His grace and His love. Otherwise, how we see is distorted.

Every time I put my glasses on, whether I've had them off for six hours or two minutes, I have to readjust. My brain reverts to the tendency to compensate. It's like that with us. Anytime we stop looking through the prism of the Word and grace and mercy, our brain will try to compensate, a task for which it is completely inept.

Look through His praise. Look through His Word. Look through His grace. Look through His love!

"In whose case the god of this world has blinded the minds
of the unbelieving so that they might not see the light of the
gospel of the glory of Christ, who is the image of God."
2 Corinthians 4:4

"'Now hear this, O foolish and senseless people,
Who have eyes but do not see;
Who have ears but do not hear.'"
Jeremiah 5:21

163

Moving from Reflection to Anticipation

As you reflect on the perceived wins and losses of your life, don't become so enamored with the process of analysis that you hold your backward glance for longer than you should.

It is good to remember, to find My purpose in places that you did not perceive in the midst of battle and pain. It is good to allow yourself time and space to evaluate missteps where you now have clarity. It is good to be grateful to Me and to the ones in your life who helped to hold up your arms when you could not sustain the energy to do so alone. And it is good to recognize the plots of the enemy, so as not to allow him the opportunity or open door in the future.

Take all this and look forward. Adjust your focus from the rearview mirror to the windshield in front of you. Bring forward the strategies, the lessons learned, and the previously-gained wisdom into a new and hope-filled future. *"Hope deferred makes the heart sick, but when desire is fulfilled, it is a tree of life"* (Proverbs 13:2).

Mix your faith with the dream that I have placed in your heart and mind, and at just the right time, I will bring it to pass. Use the sword of My word to rightly divide what desires are of Me from what desires are from your own soul.

As you look ahead, don't only see from the limitations of the front windshield, but ride on top of the vehicle; you're not driving anyway! Riding inside gives you only a narrow view. You are hampered from examining and identifying surroundings and circumstances. You are nervous to leave the safety of the transport, but hear the request of Peter to Jesus: call me out of the boat!

Allow Me to give you oversight - to see from a higher perspective. This outlook will give you understanding of the big picture, the nuances of moving pieces of the puzzle that is this season of your life. When you rise in vision with Me, you lean into My presence and rely on My voice as I speak and reveal both the seen and unseen realms.

Take My hand and let's step into the future!

"I press on toward the goal to win the [heavenly] *prize*
of the upward call of God in Christ Jesus."
Philippians 3:14 AMP

"'For I know the plans that I have for you,' declares the Lord,
'plans for prosperity and not for disaster, to give you a future and a hope.'"
Jeremiah 29:11

164

Come Up Higher

Here I am, kneeling at the steps, bowing my heart before You in worship, acknowledging Your holiness. Setting my world down and giving complete reverence to You, trusting You and Your saving power.

As I sit at the stairs put before me, I know I am on the climb. Not in striving or in trying harder, but in hearing Your call to come up higher.

My feet are unsteady as I rise off my knees to stand before You. Even as I feel weak just in that initial motion, I sense Your hands reach out immediately to take my arm.

With Your support, I take a step forward in faith, knowing You won't let go. You won't leave me hanging. So, I take a step higher following Your voice and listening for Your direction.

"Seek more of his strength! Seek more of him!
Let's always be seeking the light of his face."
Psalms 105:4 TPT

"After this I looked, and behold, a door standing open in heaven!
And the first voice which I had heard, like the sound of a [war]
trumpet speaking with me, said, 'Come up here, and I will
show you what must take place after these things.'"
Revelation 4:1 AMP

Y ou've always suspected it's true. You've considered it many times but didn't want to walk in pride, so you set it aside. But I'm confirming it to you: You're different from others.

I set you aside from your beginning. I placed you in a safe environment and I protected you. I put My Spirit in you early when you heard Me calling to you. I put things in you from your start that I'm just now calling out of you. These things – gifts and callings – I've nurtured and fed and cultivated and grown. Slowly we've pulled them up and out of you over your lifetime. But we're accelerating. Our pace is increasing, as is the depth of your gifting and its operation in My kingdom.

You've experienced seasons of loneliness where I use every opportunity to speak into you, to massage those unique gifts and to mold them for My ultimate purpose. You find yourself at the end of a night of rainstorms and overcast skies. But look up, Child, the clouds are clearing to reveal a beautiful blue heavenly sky where your vision is unobstructed, and your possibilities are endless.

Yes, you are different, unique, special, set apart, called, gifted, and chosen. Walk in your true identity as I propel you forward.

"For he knew all about us before we were born
and he destined us from the beginning
to share the likeness of his Son. This means the Son is the oldest among

a vast family of brothers and sisters who will become just like him.
Having determined our destiny ahead of time,
he called us to himself and transferred his perfect righteousness
to everyone he called. And those who possess his perfect righteousness
he co-glorified with his Son!"
Romans 8:29-30 TPT

"You didn't choose me. I chose you. I appointed
you to go and produce lasting fruit,
so that the Father will give you whatever you ask for, using my name."
John 15:16 NLT

"Being one body and one spirit,
as you were all called into the same glorious hope of divine destiny."
Ephesians 4:4 TPT

"You are not forgotten, for you have been chosen and destined by Father God.
The Holy Spirit has set you apart to be God's holy ones,
obedient followers of Jesus Christ who have been
gloriously sprinkled with his blood.
May God's delightful grace and peace cascade over you many times over!"
1 Peter 1:2 TPT

166

The Way of Escape

I see people trapped in religion, people chained and bound by the trappings of tradition. People who have become so entrenched in the sacraments they have lost sight of the point: faith in Jesus. They are literally blinded to truth and unable to escape the formulas of their minds.

They strive to set things in order in their hearts, but they are spinning like a hamster on a wheel, while creating a web they cannot see through that eventually becomes a habitation of confusion and fear.

From outside this cage of religion, others are confused as to why anyone would want to stay. People outside easily see the gate to freedom and point it out to the one entangled there. Because of the scales covering his eyes, he is unable to distinguish the opening from the walls and trinkets he's used to decorate his spiritual home.

Loved ones call out and encourage him, announcing truth, singing forth the way of escape. But he is unable to hear, distracted by a cacophony of voices, sounds, and static (all designed as a grand distraction).

So, what is the result?

We continue to sow seeds of truth. Continue to till the soil of hearts with prayer, tearing down strongholds in the spirit. Continue to sing out the joy of salvation and freedom in Christ. Continue to cast the net and invite all who will come to drink of the well of salvation. Don't grow weary in well-doing. Build yourself up on your most holy faith. Stand and see the salvation of our God.

"I would have despaired unless I had believed
that I would see the goodness of the Lord
In the land of the living."
Psalms 27:13

"It was for this freedom that Christ set us free [completely liberating us];
therefore keep standing firm and do not be subject again to a yoke of slavery
[which you once removed]."
Galatians 5:1 AMP

167

New Wine

My child, you are carrying new wine with power and freedom. I trust you as a vessel to My beloved people. I know as their Shepherd how I love them and want only their best. To trust you as a vessel means that I know your heart and trust you to love, feed, and minister to My people.

I will lead you. No need to panic at the overwhelming responsibility. You hear My voice and follow My lead.

But your vessel is ever-changing. I'm constantly molding you and adding layers of beauty, depth, discernment, and wisdom for you to share. No need to fret over the cracks or scars on your vessel. You're a container for My presence. I've sealed Myself in you and covered any area that you feel is weak. Lean into Me. Trust Me, and I will use you beyond what you could have imagined.

"No one puts new wine into old wineskins; otherwise the [fermenting] *wine will* [expand and] *burst the skins, and the wine is lost as well as the wineskins. But new wine must be put into new wineskins."*
Mark 2:22 AMP

"Listen carefully, I am about to do a new thing,
Now it will spring forth;
Will you not be aware of it?
I will even put a road in the wilderness,
Rivers in the desert."
Isaiah 43:19 AMP

"But now, O Lord, You are our Father,
We are the clay, and You our potter;
And all of us are the work of Your hand."
Isaiah 64:8

168

Contend For It

God recently confirmed a prophetic word that had been given to us in exactly the timeline the word had stated.

We were in a season of difficulty when this word was given and, immediately, our heart took hold of its promise. The word was encouraging, but definitely bold and courageous.

In the days that followed, we thought about its potential and received its truth. But then we took it a step forward and mixed our faith with it. This was not a hard thing for us to do because we had been here before: seeing God confirm and bring to pass a prophetic word. (The house we currently live in came through a word from God on many layers!)

There wasn't a smooth path between receiving this current prophetic word and its coming to fruition. I expected a steady climb toward it. However, our situation became more challenging and the temptation to doubt became more alluring.

I think it's like that many times: God brings a word, we join in with faith, then the enemy ramps up his attack to try to dissuade us from believing. (Think parable of the sower in Matthew 13:5-7.) In that interim time is the real battle: believe God, believe that the word is from God, or throw the word aside and fight our battles on our own.

This is a battle worth fighting – but in the power of His might. Feed on the written word of God and let Him confirm the rhema word, the living word, we've received. Then activate our faith and believe. Stand. Pray the word, meditate on the word, declare and contend for it.

*"And God confirmed the message by giving signs and wonders
and various miracles and gifts of the Holy Spirit whenever He chose."*
Hebrews 2:4 NLT

*"Dearly loved friend, I was fully intending to write to you about
our amazing salvation we all participate in, but felt the need
instead to challenge you to vigorously defend and contend for
the beliefs that we cherish. For God, through the apostles, has
once for all entrusted these truths to his holy believers."*
Jude 1:3 TPT

169

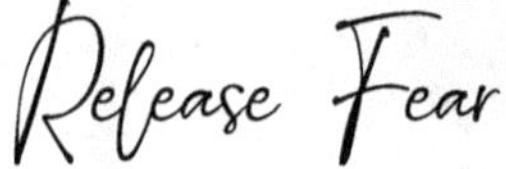

I know you're hurting, and I can sense you retreating into yourself. You think I am uncaring and less than responsive to your situation and your need.

Because you think I am not responding or moving on your behalf, you are pulling back. You are trying to say all the right things and put your heart in the correct posture, but it is less than sincere. You are acting out of obedience, but not out of intimacy with Me.

You're trying not to cross any lines, careful not to offend Me, lest I punish you by not rescuing you or setting your circumstances in order. You are standing in complete fear:

> fear of your situation,
> fear of sabotaging My response,
> fear of giving up hope,
> fear of doubting,
> fear that I won't come through.

You read all the promises in the Word, and you try to hold on to them. You're trying to move them from your head and into full belief in your heart. You are there. Stop striving and second-guessing. Trust.

"Trust in the Lord completely, and do not rely on your own opinions.
With all your heart rely on him to guide you,
and he will lead you in every decision you make.
Become intimate with him in whatever you do,
and he will lead you wherever you go."
Proverbs 3:5 TPT

170

Nose Rings

As I was contemplating my life's mission one evening, the enemy whispered, "you will never have another original thought." And just as I started to lament the possibility, Holy Spirit answered so clearly, "You don't need an original thought, you need a God thought!"

How many times do we go in circles with our own thoughts, from our own flesh, that don't lead to life? They are like a ring in the nose of a giant bull that allows him to be led in any direction the leader desires. The bull can be stronger, bigger, faster, but he has no power over the one who leads him by the nose. I too, have been led around in circles, wanting to get off the path that led to nowhere, simply because I was following my own thoughts of waste and destruction.

I desire to be led by the thoughts of God that lead to real transforming life!

I have authority in life that has been given to me by Jesus, the creator of all life! But if I lay down my authority to agree with an enemy who wants to subdue and control me, then I have willingly submitted to his dominion.

I can cry out and ask God to rescue me, and He will rescue me, but it will be by empowering me to stand in the authority I already have. I must choose to take the ring out of my nose (allegorically speaking, of course) and stop believing and agreeing with my enemy. His grace will enable me to move off this path, but I must believe Him and take a step so that He has something with which to partner. We do the thing in the natural, and He adds the super. Just as God asked Moses, "What do you have in your hand?" He is saying to us, "Give me something to work with." When Moses stretched out the staff in his hand, God did the miraculous with it. He will do the same for us!

Let's stand up and remove the ring of lies and deception that the enemy is feeding us daily. Let's stop listening to his whispers, leading us into doubt and self-recrimination. Let's stop relying on our attempts to problem solve and listen for Holy Spirit's voice of truth.

"Now you understand that I have imparted to you
my authority to trample over his kingdom.
You will trample upon every demon before you and
overcome every power Satan possesses.
Absolutely nothing will harm you as you walk in this authority."
Luke 10:19 TPT

"We are destroying sophisticated arguments
and every exalted and proud thing
that sets itself up against the [true] knowledge of God,
and we are taking every thought and purpose
captive to the obedience of Christ,"
2 Corinthians 10:5 AMP

"He has rescued us completely from the tyrannical rule of darkness
and has translated us into the kingdom realm of his beloved Son."
Colossians 1:13 TPT

171

A New Season

This is a season of new for you: new revelation, deeper revelation and understanding of Me, My ways, and My words.

You've seen and heard the phrase, "season's greetings." This will mean something unique and special to you because I, Myself, am greeting you this season with a fresh sparkle in My eye and a new vision for you.

I am bringing things together. As a puzzle comes together slowly, without the picture to use as a reference, it is a mystery what the finished craft will look like. You've been adding pieces to a puzzle without a reference. But as a wise builder, you've started with the framework. And now as you continue, I am providing new pieces! As you add them, you will see an image form that will guide you into a revelation of the puzzle's design.

I am creating a masterpiece! Not a square project where pieces are put into place and don't move, but a living, breathing, ever-changing, ever-growing masterpiece called My church. It will shift, like waves on the sea, as the ebb and flow of My Spirit brings leading and guidance.

Be encouraged! Don't grow weary in well-doing. Look to My word, for I will surely do it. Lean into Me and see My vision take shape!

"Let us not grow weary or become discouraged in doing good,
for at the proper time we will reap, if we do not give in."
Galatians 6:9 AMP

"Though your beginning was insignificant,
Yet your end will increase greatly."
Job 8:7

"I will bless my people and their homes around my holy hill.
And in the proper season I will send the showers they need.
There will be showers of blessing."
Ezekiel 34:26 NLT

172

Go Out and Come In

There is a place designed especially for you to move between your current residence and the realm of the Spirit. It is necessary for us to navigate this tension between these two worlds. Though we live this temporary life in the flesh, we receive instruction, impartation, revelation, and power from the eternal.

As we are seated with Him in heavenly places, we are also (for a fleeting lifetime) bringing Him into the earth's realm. As we re-present Him here, we draw others to His love and His provision of real, lasting life.

We must go out and come in! Just as kings of old would lead their troops to "go out" to battle and "come in" to receive rest and provision, we are to do the same.

We come in to our eternal residence in the Spirit. It is here that we receive real sustenance and all that is needed to run our race in the earth. But to exist in the Spirit and ignore the call of our lives in the earth would render us completely ineffective here. It is only through our connection to and our walk with Holy Spirit as we "come in" that we are equipped and empowered to "go out."

We must "go out," in a manner of speaking, to take what is in the Spirit and share it in the world. It is only then that we can pour out all He's given to us. We go forward proclaiming His truth and advancing the kingdom. This is our battle, to bring the Spirit into the flesh. Our purpose in this life is to add to the kingdom.

*"The Lord will guard your going out and your coming in
from this time forth and forever."*
Psalms 121:8

*"Blessed shall you be when you come in, and
blessed shall you be when you go out."*
Deuteronomy 28:6

*"I am the door; if anyone enters through Me, he will be saved,
and will go in and out and find pasture."*
John 10:9

173

In some areas of your life, you are waiting for conditions (circumstances) to become perfect before stepping out, or into, an assignment. Instead of looking with your fleshly eyes to perceive the times, look with your spiritual eyes.

Each of your physical senses is a mirror, a reflection, of a spiritual awareness that I've put within you. *"O taste and see that the Lord is good"* (Psalms 34:8a).

Ask Me to show you. When the time is right, I will declare to you, "the conditions are favorable," regardless of what you see in the natural. You will both hear My voice and see that the time is ripe for your shift and for My partnered maneuver with you.

Regardless I won't leave you hanging. Even if you over-anticipate and find yourself with a precarious foothold, feeling like you're on the precipice of disaster. *"…I will uphold you with My righteous right hand"* (Isaiah 41:10b). Even if you falter in your next step and retreat, I will not leave you, but will sustain and encourage you.

Today, I am saying, "The conditions are favorable for My unveiling and advancement!"

"Do not fear, for I am with you;
Do not anxiously look about you, for I am your God.
I will strengthen you, surely I will help you,

Surely I will uphold you with My righteous right hand.
For I am the Lord your God, who upholds your right hand,
Who says to you, 'Do not fear, I will help you.'"
Isaiah 41:10, 13

"With you as my strength I can crush an enemy horde,
advancing through every stronghold that stands in front of me.
Yahweh, what a perfect God you are!
All Yahweh's promises have proven true.
What a secure shelter for all those
who turn to hide themselves in you,
the wraparound God.
Could there be any other god like Yahweh?
For there is not a more secure foundation than you."
Psalms 18:29-31 TPT

174

Sickle

In my mind, I saw the word *sickle*. I instantly became intrigued by it and wondered what God was trying to convey to me in this word. A sickle is a gathering hook used for harvesting. It is a curved metal blade attached to a short wooden handle.

Revelation 14:14 describes Jesus sitting atop a white cloud with a crown on His head and a sharp sickle in His hand. The crown confirms his kingship, and the sickle is a tool, implying that there is a new assignment for Him to complete.

It is interesting that John describes the sickle as sharp. Wouldn't we all assume a harvesting tool would be sharp, so as to cut the ready crop? The meaning of *sharp* is more than a description of the tool's blade. It means *keen, swift, quick or rapid*. The harvesting device in the hand of Jesus is supernaturally efficient to accomplish the gathering.

Revelation 14:15-16 says an angel came out from the temple and cried out with a loud voice to him saying, *"Put in your sickle and reap, for the hour to reap has come, the harvest of the earth is ripe."* Then Jesus *"swung His sickle over the earth, and the earth was reaped."* Now, that's a sharp sickle.

The point I believe God was showing me is that the sickle is a hand tool, specifically one with a short handle, requiring the reaper to stand right beside His harvest. He stands close enough to see each shoot as He draws it to Himself, to smell the scent of the produce, and to hear the swoosh of the blade as it cuts through the stalks.

Jesus doesn't call us from afar or draw us from a distance. He stands right beside us, close enough to whisper His love and rejoice over us with singing.

If we don't know Jesus, He's not up in some far away heaven calling out our name. He's right beside us, on the other side of a thin veil, within arm's reach, seeing us, hearing us, inviting us to receive Him, and to give us life.

"Then I looked, and behold, a white cloud, and sitting on the cloud was one like a son of man, having a golden crown on His head and a sharp sickle in His hand. And another angel came out of the temple, crying out with a loud voice to Him who sat on the cloud, 'Put in your sickle and reap, for the hour to reap has come, because the harvest of the earth is ripe.' Then He who sat on the cloud swung His sickle over the earth, and the earth was reaped."
Revelation 14:14-16

"Behold, I stand at the door and knock; if anyone hears My voice and opens the door, I will come in to him and will dine with him, and he with Me."
Revelation 3:20

175

You are looking for a line to distinguish between your efforts and where I take over, but that line does not take into account the grace of empowerment and anointing. It does not mean that you stop and sit down when you discern some imaginary line.

To thread a needle requires precision, vision, acuity, steadiness, the visual ability to resolve fine detail, and quick penetrating intelligence.

You are in a season that requires vision, precision, steadiness, and acuity. You'll need the visual ability to resolve fine detail and quick penetrating intelligence. Acuity sharpness, keenness of thought, vision and hearing.

I work through men, so I need your hands and your mouth. It means that we are partners. I will enable you to do far more than you are able.

Stand fast and see through the mess and see true purpose and true destination.

"I know that You can do all things,
And that no purpose of Yours can be thwarted."
Job 42:2

"The Lord has made everything for its own purpose."
Proverbs 16:4a

"Many plans are in a man's mind,
But it is the Lord's purpose for him that will stand [be carried out]."
Proverbs 19:21 AMP

176

Come On In

I see you there, hiding behind the curtain. In the room where I dwell, I invite you in. You are welcome here. I expose the fullness of My presence, My glory, My sovereignty, My penetrating light.

I've called you into this holy sanctuary to experience all that I have for you. Through My death and resurrection, I tore the veil that left you out. I opened My home to you and bid you to enter.

But in your fear and your circumspection, you crouch down behind the very curtain that I destroyed for you. You peek inside the great room, knowing that your healing lies within the folds of My presence.

In glimpsing the vastness of My majesty, you're afraid that by stepping in I'll expose the worst of you to embarrass or humiliate you before Me. Oh child, My heart is never to put your weakness on display – but to bring healing in every part of you.

My light shines not to uncover you but to clothe you in its transforming power. I am here to bring you full, abundant, more-than-enough life, to help you cast out your imperfections and stand, fully accepted and fully healed.

Come on in. Let Me love you into complete restoration and freedom!

"And now we are brothers and sisters in God's
family because of the blood of Jesus,
and he welcomes us to come into the most holy sanctuary in
the heavenly realm—boldly and without hesitation. For he has
dedicated a new, life-giving way for us to approach God.
For just as the veil was torn in two, Jesus' body was torn open to give us
free and fresh access to him! And since we now
have a magnificent High Priest
to welcome us into God's house, we come closer to God
and approach him with an open heart, fully convinced
that nothing will keep us at a distance from him.
For our hearts have been sprinkled with blood to remove impurity,
and we have been freed from an accusing conscience.
Now we are clean, unstained, and presentable to God inside and out!"
Hebrews 10:19-22 TPT

177

Clear Direction

"Do not drive through smoke." This was written on a single sign in the hills of Oklahoma. This reminded me of NASCAR for some reason.

In a race, each driver has a headset through which he hears the voice of one person from his pit crew - usually his "spotter." This person's job is to give the driver information about things happening on the track that he cannot see for himself. Many times, he warns the driver of something that has happened in front of him that he is coming upon, giving him instruction as to how to best maneuver through obstacles that have appeared on the track.

The driver has a choice to make each time he hears the "voice in his ear." He can follow the direction of his guide, or he can make his own decisions based on his limited view and perspective from inside his car.

We can all see the wisdom of the driver following the voice in his ear. But the decision to do so comes out of real trust and relationship. When there's a wreck ahead and the view of the track is completely obscured by smoke, the natural inclination of the driver is to pump the breaks and search out the hazards. It is at that critical moment that the guide speaks his clear charge, "Go low; give it the gas, and drive through! Go, go, go!"

The insight, the perspective, and the clarity of vision of the commander gives him the unique ability to direct his driver safely through the circumstance. But ultimately, the driver follows because the guide has demonstrated his care of the driver in the past and proven himself trustworthy. The driver hears his voice, recognizes him, and follows out of faith, confidence, and an expectation of complete success.

We have the same choice. Stop at the first sign of "smoke" or keep driving and follow the direction of the "Guide" in our ear.

Obviously, the driver's spotter isn't perfect. But we have a Guide who is infallible. His love for us is without bounds, and He sees our path from a holy perspective. Without doubt, we can know that He is good, and He directs us from His perfect position.

Let's take our focus off the foggy track and put our trust in His direction.

"You will keep in perfect and constant peace the one whose mind is steadfast
[that is, committed and focused on You—
in both inclination and character],
Because he trusts and takes refuge in You
[with hope and confident expectation]."
Isaiah 26:3 AMP

178

Limitless Supply

P en in hand and your ear to your heart.

You are well able. I've spent a lifetime equipping you. Not with tools and talents, but with My presence and My spirit.

Don't mistake your lack or perceived shortage as a sign that you're unqualified for your present assignment. If you'll allow Me, I will lead you every step and I will personally fill in the gaps.

Bring your concerns to Me and turn them over. Submit your requests to Me as you see tasks and needs arise. I will not abandon you to your own devices, as we both know that your devices are limited. But My supply is endless, and I will pour it out on you with abundance. Trust Me in this and we'll both celebrate My goodness.

You are on the cusp. I've prepared a beautiful tree just for you, lush and full. It's starting to shake, and all kinds of fruit are beginning to fall from the tree. It is ripe and ready; the fruit is juicy and ready to be consumed. There is no picking required, just receiving.

You are right at the point of everything I promised breaking open. And when I break it open for you, there will be great fruit, and enough juice for everyone. Some will eat the fruit, and some will only sample the juice.

But be patient. My supply is plenty, limitless, enough for anyone who seeks to partake. Like a fruit being cut for the children: ripe, healthy, sweet, and

ready to be consumed. You won't have to work for it – no cooking required!
Just taste and see that I am good.

"O taste and see that the Lord is good; How blessed
is the man who takes refuge in Him!
O fear the Lord, you His saints; For to those who fear Him there is no want.
The young lions do lack and suffer hunger; But they who
seek the Lord shall not be in want of any good thing."
Psalms 34:8-10

"I am convinced that my God will fully satisfy every need you have,
for I have seen the abundant riches of glory
revealed to me through Jesus Christ!"
Philippians 4:19 TPT

"He's the one who brings peace to your borders,
feeding you the most excellent of fare."
Psalms 147:14 TPT

"Now may the God of peace [the source of serenity and spiritual well-being]
who brought up from the dead our Lord Jesus,
the great Shepherd of the sheep,
through the blood that sealed and ratified the eternal covenant,
equip you with every good thing to carry out His will and strengthen you
[making you complete and perfect as you ought to be], *accomplishing in us*
that which is pleasing in His sight, through Jesus Christ,
to whom be the glory forever and ever. Amen."
Hebrews 13:20-21 AMP

179

Transformers

The Intercessor:
Folded hands and praying hearts
On rugged knees of steel,
This is a real world changer;
Battling with fervent zeal.

The Worshipper:
The one who ministers in song
Leading the charge with cries;
God honors his sacrifice of praise
With grace's holy prize.

The Giver:
There's one who shares his faith
By a life well-lived in love;
His journey is marked by generosity
He can never give enough.

The Encourager:
Encouragement flows by the one sincere;
He seeks to inspire and build.
His goal is to strengthen and uplift.
To see the Church fulfilled.

The Servant:
There's one who serves others without motive
A selfless hero his name to be.
His work in the world is priceless
An honorable standard we see.

The Invitation:
The Kingdom expands and Jesus made known
When we share the gifts He imparts.
God's working through us both night and day
When we believe and give Him our hearts!

180

Cultivate

"He who cultivates his land will have plenty of bread,
but he who follows worthless people,
and frivolous pursuits will have plenty of poverty."
Proverbs 28:19 AMP

I am not a farmer, but I can appreciate tilling, planting, tending, and harvesting. On a practical level, this verse is obvious. It goes hand-in-hand with 2 Thessalonians 3:10b, *"if anyone is not willing to work, then he is not to eat, either."*

But the word of God is so rich and full that this verse also applies in layers. Understanding that the Bible is written in allegorical language pushes us to dig out the other meanings that Holy Spirit is speaking to us through the Word. He reveals all truth to us (John 16:13) just as Jesus taught parables and then explained them to his disciples.

The word "cultivates" in this verse is the Hebrew word "abad" and, 78% of the time, it is translated "serve." The question then becomes, "what is my land to serve?" I believe my land is my work, my areas of responsibility, my territory or metron of authority. The word "land" is "adama" meaning, soil, land, territory, or country.

Ultimately, I'm left with the question, "am I serving my territory, or am I following empty pursuits?" According to this Word, following frivolous pursuits or worthless people will leave me with "plenty of poverty."

Wow! How does one have plenty of poverty? If poverty is being in lack, then how can I have enough lack?

The answer lies in the definition of "plenty." In Hebrew, it is "saba," meaning "to be satisfied." When we pursue careless, pointless, empty activity, then we will become satisfied with lack in our lives. We will not only experience not enough, but we will become complacent and even comfortable in a purposeless, inadequate existence.

When I experience shortage or insufficiency in any area of my life, I must ask myself, "how have I been cultivating, tending, and serving in that area?" If I'm experiencing a lack of peace, how am I digging into my faith in my mind and emotions? If I'm experiencing a lack of provision, what or how do I sow in my finances in order to reap a different or better harvest? If I am unsatisfied in a relationship, how am I pouring into that relationship?

Without this introspection and diligence, we will find ourselves in a drab, unproductive life without meaning and nourishment. Instead of distracting ourselves with screens and devices, let's be intentional about how we invest in the areas of our lives where we experience lack. Let's determine not to be satisfied with merely being present, but to be diligent to serve. Let's never again be satisfied with "plenty of poverty"!

"Do not be deceived, God is not mocked; for whatever
a man sows, this he will also reap.
Let us not lose heart in doing good, for in due time
we will reap if we do not grow weary."
Galatians 6:7, 9

"Now this I say, he who sows sparingly will also reap sparingly,
and he who sows bountifully will also reap bountifully."
2 Corinthians 9:6

181

I'm bringing you into a new season of revelation! I will show you deep and mysterious things. You won't always be called to share what you've seen, but what I've revealed to you in what you've seen. Look thoroughly at what I'm showing you for every detail of the message.

You are to scatter seed! You are a broadcaster!

I have put My seed in you. Not just one seed, but an endless supply of seed. And I have equipped you to scatter My seed, My living Word. You are ready. You've been tentative to fully take hold of your tools. It is time to put your hand to the holy tool I have designed just for you: a broadcaster.

I'm adding directional fins that I'll use to show you the area where you will sow in this new season. Those directions will be subject to change at a moment's notice, so be vigilant and always attentive to the variations of My leading.

All broadcast spreaders require some form of power to spin. I am your source. If you go in a direction, moving effectively and productively, don't disengage from Me and try continuing on your own. Initially, the inertia will carry you forward, but you'll become unproductive. Soon you'll find yourself pushing and pulling instead of spreading the seed I've given you.

Your tools are fully functional. Once you pull from the resource of My full supply, I will bring forth the right seed at the right time, and you will scatter them. Yours isn't to produce the crop. I will bring the increase.

"So let's not get tired of doing what is good.
At just the right time we will reap a harvest of blessing if we don't give up."
Galatians 6:9 NLT

Now, go and scatter My seed!

"Now He who supplies seed to the sower and
bread for food will supply and multiply
your seed for sowing and increase the harvest of your righteousness."
2 Corinthians 9:10

"Here, then, is the deeper meaning to my parable:
The word of God is the seed that is sown into hearts."
Luke 8:11 TPT

182

Seed, Time, and Harvest

The Bible has many references to farming that teach us God's principles: Seed, time, and harvest, the parable of the different kinds of ground, etc. Our worship is like plowing the ground of our hearts.

What's the purpose of plowing? Most of us relate to plowing before planting. It's preparing the ground to receive something, a seed. Plowing is necessary to break up the hard places. Many farmers also plow after a harvest. This starts the breakdown process of moving organic materials into the soil. A field that's been plowed after harvest works up nicer than one that's only plowed in the spring before a planting season.

The benefit of plowing is that it allows moisture to filter into the soil instead of running off. The runoff does the field no good; it only creates ruts and ditches that invite the water to return the next time, growing deeper with each runoff. A great rain can come, but the ruts and ditches divert the nourishing water from the plants for which it was intended.

I want to enter into worship ready to plow some ground. I want to join with God and see the places He's breaking up, or preparing, or watering, or planting new seed, or nourishing.

"I said, 'Plant the good seeds of righteousness,
and you will harvest a crop of love.
Plow up the hard ground of your hearts,
for now is the time to seek the Lord,
that he may come and shower righteousness upon you.'"
Hosea 10:12 NLT

"See, I care about you, and I will pay attention to you.
Your ground will be plowed and your crops planted."
Ezekiel 36:9 NLT

"This is what the Lord says to the people of Judah and Jerusalem:
'Plow up the hard ground of your hearts!
Do not waste your good seed among thorns.'"
Jeremiah 4:3 NLT

183

My very nature is multiplication. When I speak, My words create and continue forward. I am declaring multiplication over you, your life, your ministry, and the work of your hands.

You are only limited by your own failure to sow. What is in your hand? I will grow it! Prepare for it! Make space for multiplication!

As I instructed the widow through Elisha, go and gather all the empty jars you can find (2 Kings 4:3). Gather the empty vessels and I will fill them.

What are the vessels I'm asking you to gather? What do your jars look like?

They could be quiet moments of listening for My voice.

They could be lingering worship instead of plowing ahead to the next item on your agenda.

They could be foregoing a good opportunity while keeping an availability for a God-sized one.

Your jars could look like songs and extended prayer and barefoot walks.

Your jars could look like free days on a busy calendar.

Your jars could look like rainy Saturday afternoons with your Bible and your journal.

Your jars could look like a conference with an expectation for a move of Holy Spirit.

They could look like tears and renewal and changing
your mind.

Don't focus on the perceived limited supply of oil coming from the natural source. Keep your eyes on the provision flowing into the empty containers. I am filling up hearts and minds and homes and lives. I will pour My very Spirit out and fill them to the top!

"One day the widow of a member of the group of prophets came to Elisha and cried out, 'My husband who served you is dead, and you know how he feared the Lord. But now a creditor has come, threatening to take my two sons as slaves.' 'What can I do to help you?' Elisha asked. 'Tell me, what do you have in the house?' 'Nothing at all, except a flask of olive oil,' she replied. And Elisha said, 'Borrow as many empty jars as you can from your friends and neighbors. Then go into your house with your sons and shut the door behind you. Pour olive oil from your flask into the jars, setting each one aside when it is filled.' So she did as she was told. Her sons kept bringing jars to her, and she filled one after another. Soon every container was full to the brim! 'Bring me another jar,' she said to one of her sons. 'There aren't any more!' he told her. And then the olive oil stopped flowing. When she told the man of God what had happened, he said to her, 'Now sell the olive oil and pay your debts, and you and your sons can live on what is left over.'"

2 Kings 4:1-7 NLT

184

Speak Life

Words in my mouth like pebbles spilling out. In my mouth, they sit without power, like fish swimming in a fishbowl, confined, limited, and circling around with no effect.

But by Your spirit, You form them in my mouth and empower them as I speak them into the atmosphere. And then everything changes. Because as You empower me to speak, You bring life to my spoken word when it is in alignment with Your Word. Your creative power comes alive by my word.

Put Your word in my mouth. All else is nonsense. Errant words spoken foolishly carry no power. Why would I waste opportunity when I've been given the ability to bring life?

Speak, prophesy to dry, dead bones, and bring life!

"A word fitly spoken and in due season is like
apples of gold in settings of silver."
Proverbs 25:11 AMP

"Then said the Lord to me, 'You have seen well, for I am [actively]
watching over My word to fulfill it.'"
Jeremiah 1:12 AMP

185

Unseen Fruit

I am changing lives. You sometimes doubt that your efforts to further the kingdom are producing enough results. You question yourself, your call, and your impact.

I am partnered with you, enabling you, sustaining you, and empowering you to fight the good fight. There is fruit from your ministry that you've never seen, and some you will never see. The fact that you don't see it doesn't diminish its existence or its relevance.

There is also fruit that looks completely different from what you expected to see. The tree of life in the garden bore the fruit of life, but your mind can't comprehend what that must've looked like. I am still producing life!

My encouragement for you is the message of momentum. I have already begun a good work in you, and I am ramping up the momentum of its progress. I am propelling you forward into a season of great impact for Me. The impetus and incitement in this season is My word. You'll be drawn and compelled by its truth to a new level and degree.

Don't let your intentions be so result-centered that you compromise My direction. You elevate Me and My kingdom, and I will draw men to myself.

Stay in step with Me as we move forward: bigger, higher, stronger, faster. I will produce. You stay connected to Me, and you will bear fresh, plump, ripened, sweet fruit, both seen and yet unseen.

"*The righteous will flourish like the date palm* [long-lived, upright and useful]; *they will grow like a cedar in Lebanon* [majestic and stable]. *Planted in the house of the Lord, they will flourish in the courts of our God.* [Growing in grace] *they will still thrive and bear fruit and prosper in old age; they will flourish and be vital and fresh* [rich in trust and love and contentment]; [they are living memorials] *to declare that the Lord is upright and faithful* [to His promises]; *He is my rock, and there is no unrighteousness in Him.*"
Psalms 92:12-15 AMP

"*Every branch in Me that does not bear fruit, He takes away; and every branch that continues to bear fruit, He* [repeatedly] *prunes, so that it will bear more fruit* [even richer and finer fruit]. *You are already clean* because of the word which I have given you [the teachings which I have discussed with you]. *Remain in Me, and I* [will remain] *in you. Just as no branch can bear fruit by itself without remaining in the vine, neither can you* [bear fruit, producing evidence of your faith] *unless you remain in Me. I am the Vine; you are the branches. The one who remains in Me and I in him bears much fruit, for* [otherwise] *apart from Me* [that is, cut off from vital union with Me] *you can do nothing.*"
John 15:2-5 AMP

186

The Peak is Obscured

I look to see a collection of mountains. Each of them is beautiful on its own. If they each stood alone, my view would still be spectacular.

Looking at each mountain, my focus goes quickly to the peak. I take great delight in measuring the peaks against the sky, while also taking in each face and its glorious uniqueness. There are a few clouds that hang in the air around them. Some are dainty and transparent, while others are thicker and block my full view.

In this case, the peak that I desire to see is covered by a round cloud that completely blocks it from view. While the other clouds are rolling by or shifting their shape, this cloud sitting in the midst of the peak is thick and unmoving.

I am reminded of Solomon's temple dedication when the presence of God came in the form of a cloud. The priests could not minister by reason of the cloud. God's presence manifested in a cloud, just as it had in Moses' day when He led the nation of Israel through the wilderness. The cloud had served as both a guide and as protection for His people from the hot sun. They followed the protection.

As I contemplate the current phenomenon, God reminds me that we may not always be able to see the destination clearly, but His presence and protection will always be available. There are times that we would be completely overwhelmed if we could see the details at the apex.

In this particular instance I can clearly see the face of the mountain. Should I choose to, I have the opportunity to decide where to climb and how to make my way to the top. I believe there are circumstances that God gives us freedom and opportunity to choose a path and then walks with us along the way. Other times, He will only illuminate the next step.

In either case, we must choose to follow His voice. Whether I can clearly see the destination or not, the journey of listening and responding is the same. Do I feel more confident when I know exactly where I am going? I do. But even when I see the goal, I still have to navigate obstacles along the way.

Many times, God does not show me the peak, the ultimate objective, for my own protection. At times, it would overwhelm me and serve as counterproductive to the goal. Other times, I would be tempted to create my own way up the mountain and manipulate the circumstances for my desired progress. This sidesteps what God needs to do in me through the journey, thereby missing the character alterations that I need to make in order to operate at my intended target and be who He designed me to be when I get there.

"Your word is a lamp to my feet
And a light to my path."
Psalms 119:105

"The glory of the Lord rested on Mount Sinai,
and the cloud covered it for six days;
and on the seventh day He called to Moses from the midst of the cloud."
Exodus 24:16

My Sparkle in You

I've set My vision in your heart. With a foundation of gratitude, I'm elevating you into a position of influence – not because there is anything special about you, but because I've set My purpose upon you, and you are a willing vessel.

You are entering a season of diligence. You've reclined at the table and tasted My goodness. You've learned to receive My sustenance. You've been on a feeding frenzy! And the time has come for you to go out and come back in. Your meal won't grow stale while you answer My assignment. But do not get so caught up in the assignments that you neglect My table. Take My bread to a hungry world and have them taste and see that I am good.

We are refining your mission. I am the Master Jeweler. I've designed you as a beautiful necklace, a chain with many links. I've connected them perfectly and the time has come to buff out the layers of overcoating to reveal a shine and sparkle that has previously gone unnoticed. I am drawing the eye to My sparkle in you. Point them to Me.

Through this holy refining together we will unveil direction and focus. Be intentional in your pursuits and not lax or wasteful. There is much at stake in a hurting and desperate world; your voice is needed and welcome as a salve for searching souls.

Listen for My word, My freshly spoken rhema: This is the way; walk in it.

"Son of man, prophesy and say, 'Thus says the Lord.' Say,
'A sword, a sword sharpened
And also polished!'"
Ezekiel 21:9

"So don't hide your light! Let it shine brightly before others,
so that your commendable works will shine as light upon them,
and then they will give their praise to your Father in heaven."
Matthew 5:16 TPT

188

Say Something

You call it the ministry of reconciliation. I am saying, "I am bringing dead things to life!"

Ezekiel 37:1–14.

> *"The hand of the Lord was upon me, and He*
> *brought me out by the Spirit of the Lord*
> *and set me down in the middle of the valley; and it was full of bones.*
> *He said to me, 'Son of man, can these bones live?' And I answered,*
> *'O Lord God, You know.' Again He said to me,*
> *'Prophesy over these bones and say to them, "O*
> *dry bones, hear the word of the Lord."'*
> *So I prophesied as I was commanded; and as I prophesied, there was a noise,*
> *and behold, a rattling; and the bones came together, bone to its bone.*
> *And I looked, and behold, sinews were on them,*
> *and flesh grew and skin covered them; but there was no breath in them."*
> Ezekiel 37:1,3,4,7,8

> *"Then He said to me, 'Prophesy to the breath, prophesy...'"*
> Ezekiel 37:9a

God chooses to work in the earth through man! He could have set up His earthly principles and precepts any way He wanted. But He chooses to work through man! That is why He instructed Ezekiel to prophesy!

Prophesy!?! What does that mean? The Bible says, *"For you can all* prophesy" (1 Corinthians 14:31). We wonder, what does that even mean? I don't know what that looks like! How do I do that?

Speak life! Ezekiel spoke life and dead bleached-out, dried-up bones came back together! SPEAK LIFE!

"Then He said to me, 'Prophesy to the breath, prophesy, son of man, and say to the breath, "Thus says the Lord God, 'Come from the four winds, O breath, and breathe on these slain, that they come to life.'"' So I prophesied as He commanded me, and the breath came into them, and they came to life and stood on their feet, an exceedingly great army. Then He said to me, 'Son of man, these bones are the whole house of Israel; behold, they say, "Our bones are dried up and our hope has perished. We are completely cut off."'"
Ezekiel 37:9-11

Some of us go from day to day to day with our bones just drying up. And some of us could testify, "My hope is gone. My dream is dead. That thing I thought I was destined to do...my opportunity came and went, and I never saw it, much less seized it."

But TODAY God says to us,

"Therefore prophesy and say to them, 'Thus says the Lord God, "Behold, I will open your graves and cause you to come up out of your graves, My people; and I will bring you into the land of Israel. Then you will know that I am the Lord, when I have opened your graves and caused you to come up out of your graves, My people. I will put My Spirit within you and you will come to life, and I will place you on your own land. Then you will know that I, the Lord, have spoken and done it," declares the Lord.'"
Ezekiel 37:12-14

189

Trailblazer

When we travel to see our children in another state, we travel on a turnpike that goes through an undeveloped area. The unique thing about this highway is its elevated nature. There are hills all around the area, and the road seems to often follow the tops of the hills, providing a stunning view of the landscape.

As we returned home from a recent visit, I began to study the wooded areas below us on this stretch of thoroughfare. Initially, I was somewhat confounded by the thick woods below. But because of the current winter season, it is easy to see through the trees. I began to search for trails through the woods, evidence of experience in the areas. But just as I became enticed with this activity, I sensed the Lord correct my search.

"Penny, don't merely look for someone else's steps to follow; instead, look for the patterns of openings that I've designed to create your own trail. When you do this, you'll discover My ultimate plan for you, not just to follow in the predictable ways of others. I am making openings for you, places perfect for you to enter the lush but dense forest of this world. There are spaces and paths laid out for you that no one else has trod. These trails will be particular to you and your assignment. As you navigate them, do not look for the footprints of others to ensure that you are on the right path; I am your only guide, you've no need for a tracker to investigate the ways of others.

"When you're among the trees, they all look the same, and you cannot possibly see the small differences and minute details in the places that I've made for you to walk. The obstacles and opportunities all look the same to you. You cannot fathom the same outlook between your daily steps and My exalted point of view.

"From this angle, you can easily understand My ability to guide you from above. I am able to see what is ahead, and I will lead you to avoid undesirable areas and positions. I have shown you this viewpoint to serve as a frame of reference in the future. When circumstances seem overwhelming to you, you can remember My perspective and trust Me to move you to a place of security and rest before you have to manage another long trek through uncharted territory.

"Listen for me, follow My voice, and respond in obedience and compliance. The fulfillment of your destiny requires it!"

"Direct me, Yahweh, throughout my journey so I
can experience your plans for my life.
Reveal the life-paths that are pleasing to you."
Psalms 25:4 TPT

"Your ears will hear a word behind you, "This is the way, walk
in it," whenever you turn to the right or to the left."
Isaiah 30:21

"I hear the Lord saying, "I will stay close to you, instructing and guiding
you along the pathway for your life. I will advise you along the way and
lead you forth with my eyes as your guide. So don't make it difficult;
don't be stubborn when I take you where you've not been before.
Don't make me tug you and pull you along. Just come with me!""
Psalms 32:8-9 TPT

190

The Table of the Lord

"You prepare a table before me in the presence of my enemies;
You have anointed my head with oil; My cup overflows."
Psalms 23:5

To *prepare* means *to array, to arrange* or *lay out in order*. Even now in the midst of the trials of life, God is taking the utmost care to make arrangements, especially for you.

What is this table? It is a meal, but not just a casual meal. It is a king's table, a feast.

I used to envision this grand table with the most savory dishes and the freshest fruits, beautiful, tasty delicacies that I'd never experienced before. I limited my imagination to literal food I would consume. I've come to realize that this grand sustenance is more than meat and bread and potatoes. It is provision for my current needs and my coming battles.

The night before the children of Israel left Egypt, God started the first feast of Passover. He gave them specific instructions about the meal and said, "Eat every part!" I always thought it was just a nice family meal. But in reality, it was a much more important occasion and meal (Exodus 12).

What does it mean that He prepares it before me? He literally does it right in front of you, not hidden. It's not off in a distance or even in secret. It is in front of you, and it's especially for you.

God prepares this table in the presence of your enemies. *In their presence* means that *it's straight forward, right in their face!* God isn't hiding His preparations or His plans for your good.

One enemy is obvious: the devil (1 Peter 5:8). But there are other enemies: distresses, afflictions, adversaries, pangs (or pains). When any of these enemies are present, look for the table!

This prepared meal is not just for you to eat later in heaven, although He is preparing a place for us there. We know that the table is for today, because our enemies won't be in our face in heaven.

David said, *"I would have despaired unless I had believed that I would see the goodness of the Lord in the land of the living"* (Psalm 27:13).

Eternity doesn't mean later; it means forever; it's today.

God is giving you the tools and utensils to partake of the provision and delicacies that He is laying out for you, at the table of grace:

Glory is the estimation or the value that you give God. When you recognize that God is Who He says He is, you're able to eat from the table. When you see His splendor and His brightness, when you are faced with His majesty, you're eating from the table!

The anointing of God is an unction. When you sense His unction for you in an assignment, and when you sense His special grace on you to do something, you're eating from the table! Step into the plan He has for you and take the sustenance from the prepared meal that He has arranged just for you!

The Word says that the joy of the Lord will be your strength (Nehemiah 8:10). As you experience times of joy, don't reject them because an enemy's lying voice inside you says that you should not be feeling this because you should be sad, ever grieving. Join into those moments of rejoicing and gladness and know that they are from the table of the Lord! That joy was set out just for you!

Another word for resurrection is "raising up."

The resurrection, or coming to life, of those things believed to be gone is not only possible but designed by God. It's His very nature to restore and resurrect hopes, dreams, visions, and forgotten promises. When you're reminded of these and see them sprouting forth with the new signs of life, look for the table! These are present for you to take nourishment and partake!

The Bible says that healing is the children's bread (Mark 7: 24-30). If you are a believer, you are a child of God (Galatians 3:26-27). Healing is as much a part of God's plan for you as salvation. Healing is a basic right for the children of God as bread is for a child in the home. Even when you don't see it manifest with your physical eyes, you can still trust that it's true, and you continue to look for it and expect it. When you sense healing in emotions, you're eating from the table of the Lord. When you see healing taking place in relationships, look for the table! When you experience healing that allows you to remember with fondness and not be clouded with fear and regret, you're tasting the goodness of His meal for you! Search out this healing and anticipate its place in your life; it's your right! He already paid for it for you; it's yours!

God is even now restoring the earth, though fallen and faulty, to Himself. His plan is to restore, to make things whole again. Even as you experience an enormous hole in your heart, it is His grand desire to fill it and to heal it. It won't ever be as it was before the great sadness, because of the void that was left by a grievous loss. But with Holy Spirit salve, applied from within, your heart can begin the healing process from the inside out. This oil of Holy Spirit won't cover over or hide the loss in your heart, but He can fill it with His presence, making you whole again. As you catch the fragrance of this holy balm, look for the table of the Lord. He is surely serving you through this divine practice. Receive it and watch Him work in you.

We live in a broken and fallen world. And despite its broken state, God is ever at work to repair and rebuild for us. He is bringing our meager pieces together to renew them and create something beautiful in our lives. We cannot do the building or the mending; our job is only to offer up our brokenness and submit it to the Father. When we sacrifice our right to correct every wrong, He is free to transform the broken fragments of our hearts into a masterpiece. Be on the lookout for signs of renewal. It looks like love; it looks like peace; it looks like kindness; it looks like humility. All of these are out of the overflow of eating at His great table!

Keep eternity ever in your heart. As God reminds you of the eternal life that you have in Him, He is feeding you from His table. Even those lost from this realm who are in Christ await you in a land where there is no space or time, no separation from the Father, and no loss or pain. There is only love, and bliss, and anticipation. Bear this expectancy to be together again without malice or judgement of God, yourself, or others. Walk through this life awaiting the joy that is to come, but without limiting opportunity for the joy that He provides along the journey. Though seemingly endless and monotonous, the journey is but a vapor until the time of reunion. Live all in.

Indulge in every morsel; savor every tidbit; and relish every bite of His goodness and His luxurious feast provided for you!

"Yahweh is my best friend and my shepherd.
I always have more than enough.
He offers a resting place for me in his luxurious love.
His tracks take me to an oasis of peace near the quiet brook of bliss.
That's where he restores and revives my life.
He opens before me the right path
and leads me along in his footsteps of righteousness
so that I can bring honor to his name.
Even when your path takes me through
the valley of deepest darkness,
fear will never conquer me, for you already have!
Your authority is my strength and my peace.
The comfort of your love takes away my fear.
I'll never be lonely, for you are near.
You become my delicious feast
even when my enemies dare to fight.
You anoint me with the fragrance of your Holy Spirit;
you give me all I can drink of you until my cup overflows.
So why would I fear the future?
Only goodness and tender love pursue me all the days of my life.
Then afterward, when my life is through,
I'll return to your glorious presence to be forever with you!"
Psalms 23:1-6 TPT

About the Author

Penny has been married to Rusty for 39 years, and together they have two children, two grandchildren and three grand dogs. Penny has worked in the same position of community management for over 39 years where she fulfills a passion for serving her city and for working with teens and young adults. She especially enjoys connecting young people to the vision of their future.

She is certified as an American Red Cross Lifeguarding Instructor and Water Safety Instructor Trainer, and she has trained and managed 40 summer aquatics staffs. In 1995 she received a monumental commendation, the Lifesaving Award from the American Red Cross for performing CPR and saving a life.

Penny has served in worship for over 25 years, and she currently serves as a Worship Leader and as Elder and Care Pastor at OneChurch Whitesboro.

Penny is a natural cheerleader and is an engaging teacher. Writing gives her great pleasure and reflective insight in life. She loves sunshine, music, the ocean, and the color yellow.

Notes

Day 2, One With Him

1. Lemmel, Helen Howarth, "Turn Your Eyes Upon Jesus." 1922, Public Domain

Day 5, Cadence

2. In Aramaic this verse can be translated "He arose to be the Sabbath for the people of God."

Day 80, The Way to Peace

3. Osinachi Kalu Okoro Egbu, Sinach. *Way Maker.* Chant Down Babylon: The Island Anthology. Released June 18, 1996.

Day 86, Which One of These is Not Like the Other

4. Bob Goff: X (Twitter Post), July 23, 2015 9:48 AM

Day 117, I Am Your Source

5. https://www.coreytowe.com/2017/07/27/the-power-of-working-together/

Day 131, Strategies

6. https://biblereasons.com/temptation/. Assessed 01/12/2024

Day 149, My "Yes"

7. https://quotefancy.com/bill-johnson-quotes. Assessed 01/12/2024

8. Rewards and Motives – Bill Johnson – Bethel https://youtu.be/cbRlbhDl4d0?s;=1drbhsl6CNflBTti

Author's Note

If you desire to begin a relationship with Jesus, you can do so right now. Even as you've read His words throughout the pages of this text, He has been calling to hearts that haven't fully trusted Him to step out in faith. (*The Lord is… not wishing for any to perish but for all to come to repentance*" 2 Peter 3:9.) A relationship with Jesus is possible not because of anything we can do, but all because of what He did on our behalf. He did what we could not. (*"God saved you by his grace when you believed. And you can't take credit for this; it is a gift from God. Salvation is not a reward for the good things we have done, so none of us can boast about it*" Ephesians 2:8-9 NLT.)

We were born into a fallen world without the life of His Spirit in us. We were born without, and nothing man could do would change that. (*"Then Jesus said, 'Come to me, all of you who are weary and carry heavy burdens, and I will give you rest'*" Matthew 11:28-29 NLT.) When we call Him Lord of our life, we are declaring that we trust Him, and we put Him in the role of King. (*"For 'Everyone who calls on the name of the Lord will be saved'*" Romans 10:13 NLT.) His Holy Spirit comes to live inside us to reveal truth to us, to remind us of what God says about us, and to comfort us while we are here on this earthly home. Holy Spirit is God and becomes our communicator, sharing with us the fresh, living words of God.

We simply believe and declare, "Jesus is Lord!" (*"…and no one can say Jesus is Lord, except by the Holy Spirit*" 1 Corinthians 12:3b NLT.)

If you've taken that step today as a new Believer, I would love to encourage you and give you tools in your new walk with Christ. Contact me at www.pennyrenfroe.com.